More Praise for Dr. Karp
and
THE HAPPIEST TODDLER ON THE BLOCK

"Dr. Karp's excellent approach gives parents the tools they need. His simple methods make raising rambunctious toddlers a whole lot easier."
—*Steven P. Shelov, M.D., Editor in Chief, American Academy of Pediatrics'* Caring for Your Baby and Young Child

"Dr. Karp's approach is terrific . . . and fun!"
—*Martin Stein, M.D., Professor of Pediatrics, University of California at San Diego, Children's Hospital San Diego*

"Parents will be delighted by this clever approach to communicating with toddlers. It allows us to see the world from our children's unique point of view."
—*Janet Serwint, Professor of Pediatrics, Director of the Harriet Lane Children's Clinic, Johns Hopkins School of Medicine*

"Dr. Karp's new book is an innovative, unique, and thoroughly enjoyable guide to toddler behavior!"
—*Donald Middleton, M.D., Professor of Family Medicine, University of Pittsburgh School of Medicine*

"Dr. Karp helps parents turn the 'terrible' twos into 'terrific' twos. His work will revolutionize the way our culture understands toddlers!"
—*Roni Cohen Leiderman, Ph.D., Dean of Mailman Segal Institute for Early Childhood Studies, Nova Southeastern University*

"It really works! With great humor and a gentle touch, Dr. Karp shows how to raise happy, well-behaved toddlers. His book is invaluable."
—*Gabrielle Redford, senior editor,* AARP Magazine, *and mother of seventeen-month-old twins*

By Harvey Karp, M.D.

The Happiest Baby on the Block (book and DVD)
The Happiest Toddler on the Block (book and DVD)
The Happiest Baby Guide to Great Sleep

The
Happiest Toddler
on the Block

How to Eliminate Tantrums and
Raise a Patient, Respectful, and
Cooperative One- to Four-Year-Old
Revised Edition

Harvey Karp, M.D.

with Paula Spencer

Bantam Books

THE HAPPIEST TODDLER ON THE BLOCK
A Bantam Book

PUBLISHING HISTORY
Bantam hardcover edition published March 2004
Bantam revised hardcover and trade paperback editions /
September 2008

Published by Bantam Dell
A Division of Random House, Inc.
New York, New York

Illustration on page 15 from YOUR TWO-YEAR-OLD
by Louise Bates Ames, Ph.D., and Frances L. Ilg, copyright © 1976
by The Gesell Institute of Child Development, Frances L. Ilg and
Louise Bates Ames. Used by permission of Dell Publishing,
a division of Random House, Inc.

Illustrations copyright © 2008 by Margeaux Lucas
Book design by Virginia Norey

Bantam Books and the rooster colophon are registered trademarks
of Random House, Inc.

Library of Congress Cataloging-in-Publication Data

Karp, Harvey.
The happiest toddler on the block : how to eliminate tantrums and
raise a patient, respectful, and cooperative one- to four-year-old /
Harvey Karp ; with Paula Spencer. — Rev. ed.
p. cm.
978-0-553-80521-5 (hardcover)
978-0-553-38442-0 (trade ppbk)
1. Toddlers.   2. Child rearing.   3. Toddlers—Development.
I. Spencer, Paula.   II. Title.

HQ774.5.K37 2008
649'.122—dc22
2008015230

Printed in the United States of America
Published simultaneously in Canada

www.bantamdell.com

24 26 28 30 29 27 25 23

BVG

To all my little toddler patients, who invite me into their prehistoric world every day!

Contents

Acknowledgments

"The more things change, the more they remain the same."
—Alphonse Karr, 19th-century French journalist

Ever since I was little, I have been fascinated by trying to understand how everything in our world . . . makes sense! How all of nature dances and spins, pulls and pushes, and yet, in extraordinary and unexpected ways, always finds its way back to a perfect harmony.

In the work I did with families for nearly thirty years, I came to understand that toddlers also always "make sense"! They dance and spin, pull and push, but they can quickly be led back to harmony—if you know the path. For decades, I traveled that path every day with the toddlers who visited me for their health care. And now, like an adventurer just back from an unexplored land, I am very excited to share the secrets I have discovered about toddlers with parents, grandparents, health professionals, educators, and all others who love young children.

I have many people to thank for shining their light on my explorations and helping me to see toddlerhood in all its funny and satisfying beauty. My embryology professor at SUNY

Buffalo, Gordon Swartz, a brawny ex-boxer with a passion for teaching; Arthur H. Parmelee, Jr., my child development professor at UCLA, a kind and patient man with a deep compassion for and understanding of children; and the concise and insightful writings of Carl Rogers, Haim Ginott, Thomas Gordon, Francis Ilg, Louise Bates Ames, Adele Faber and Elaine Mazlich, Stephanie Marston, Hans Miller, and many others.

Thanks as well to my soul mate and treasured wife, Nina, for her constant love and patience, and to my daughter, Lexi, for her good nature during my long hours of distraction and absence; to my late mother, Sophie, who many years ago taught me Alphonse Karr's words and thus planted the seed for one of the pivotal underpinnings of this book; to the kindness and caring of my father, Joe, and the generous heart of my unofficial stepmother, Celia; to the superb organizing and writing talents of Paula Spencer; to the illustrious imaginations of Margeaux Lucas and C. A. Nobens; to my agent, Suzanne Gluck, who helped keep this project moving forward; and to my always thoughtful and honest editor, Beth Rashbaum, who endured my constant "what-ifs" and "why nots" with considerable (and much appreciated) diplomatic aplomb.

My appreciation also goes out to the many professionals who shared with me their insights into how to teach parents these special techniques, especially Kyle Pruett, Steven Shelov, Morris Green, Janet Serwint, Martin Stein, Roni Leiderman, Jana Clay, and Christine Schoppe Wauls.

And finally, the biggest thanks of all to the trusting parents who chose me as their children's doctor and allowed me to travel with them into the exotic and extraordinary prehistoric valleys of their toddlers' minds.

Without the help of all of you this book would not have been possible.

Introduction

How I Found the Secret to Successful Communication with Toddlers

"The real voyage of discovery consists not in seeking out new lands, but in having a new vision."

—Marcel Proust

Where did your baby go? One day you're cradling a tiny newborn in your arms, all of parenthood stretched out in front of you. Then before you know it, you're living with an all-new creature—cuter than ever, but suddenly opinionated, stubborn, and lightning fast. Welcome to toddlerhood!

Toddlerhood is one of the joyous high points of parenthood. There's nothing like a one-, two-, or three-year-old to help you see the world in wonderful new ways: the bugs in the grass . . . the shapes in the clouds . . . the "castles" in a pile of sand. Toddlers brim with curiosity, excitement, and irresistible charm.

But as every parent knows, it's not all fun. Toddlerhood is like three parts fiesta mixed with two parts wrestling match and one part jungle safari. That's why, around the first birthday, many parents experience a mini "clash of civilizations" as their toddlers' actions and opinions put them on a collision course with the rules and expectations of the family.

One big reason toddlers act so wild is because during these early years, they experience an explosive rush of brain development that frequently knocks them off balance. Between your child's first and fourth birthdays, he'll be carried on a thrilling journey, like a galloping horse ride, that will magically transform him from a wobbly, grunting (and adorable) little being into a singing, joking, thoughtful little person . . . right in front of your eyes.

Progress Has Its Price

All that progress comes at a cost—mainly in wear and tear on your back, your patience, and your sanity. Anyone living with a toddler knows how quickly the emotional climate can shift. One minute all is bliss. Then *bam!* They cry, scream, and erupt into a tantrum (often in the most embarrassing places). Despite your best intentions, it can feel like the only words that come out of your mouth are "No!" "Stop!" and "Don't touch!" And that's no fun.

No wonder questions about patience, sharing, and misbehavior top the list of concerns parents of toddlers bring to their pediatricians. The hundreds of books and thousands of articles written on the subject are clear proof that if you're having a hard time dealing with your toddler's behavior, you're not alone.

For thousands of years, countless generations of parents have struggled to get their young kids to behave. Too often, they used beating and bullying to provide the necessary discipline. Parents who didn't hit their sassy toddlers were warned that their children would grow into spoiled and rebellious youths.

Fortunately, many communities began to phase out harsh physical punishment as a parenting tool fifty years ago. However, all too often it was replaced by another very negative approach—verbal aggression. Parents commonly responded to their toddlers' undesirable behaviors with verbal attacks and threats such as "You're stupid!" or "Shut up, or I'll really give you something to cry about!"

Over the past thirty years, we have come to recognize the destructive effects of rejection and hurtful words. Gradually we began to encourage parents to answer their child's outbursts with love and reason. Unfortunately, while patient explanations and respectful words work well with big kids, this approach often flops when it comes to soothing stormy toddlers.

But if big-kid-style communication is not the answer, what can a parent do to raise a kind, cooperative toddler? Plenty! However, before you can learn what to do, you need to understand one odd but *critically* important fact. . . .

Your Toddler Is *Not* Just a Miniature Child

Toddlers are not simply miniaturized versions of older kids. Their brains are much more immature, which makes their whole way of thinking more rigid and primitive and makes their behavior quite . . . uncivilized. In fact, over the next few years, one of your top parental jobs will be to *civilize* your child: teach him to say "please" and "thank you," to wait his turn, and to pee in the potty.

The uncivilized nature of toddlers became apparent to me as a young pediatrician. At the start of my career, I followed the advice in "the books" and spoke patiently with the crying kids I was examining. But my kind words often backfired and made them scream even more! So I began trying other approaches.

I tried distraction ("Hey, look at this fun toy!"), reassurance ("See, it really tickles."), empathy ("I know you hate shots, but . . ."), and respect ("May I check if your ears are healthy inside?"). But my loving words often just bounced right off of them. I might as well have been talking Swahili for all the good it did. Despite my best attempts, too many toddler checkups ended with a *frustrated* mom holding a *frantic* child being examined by a *flustered* doctor.

Then it suddenly dawned on me—toddlers don't think like older kids . . . so why speak to them like older kids?

Compared to older children, toddlers have immature brains (no surprise there), and when they get upset the brain center that controls language, logic, and patience literally *shuts down.* No wonder they become impulsive and their behavior gets *primitive.* (FYI—the same shift happens in our adult brains when we get upset; that's why angry grown-ups rant and rave . . . and become impatient and irrational!)

Eureka! Suddenly it all made sense. It was no accident that there was a little toddler in *The Flintstones* named Bamm-Bamm. Upset toddlers spit, scratch, and yell because their stressed-out brains fall apart. In seconds, they're transformed from little *children* to a bunch of Conan the Barbarians. And, the more upset they get . . . the more uncivilized they act.

I tested out my new theory by speaking to my cranky little patients in a simpler, more primitive language (kind of like Tarzan in the movies), and I was amazed to discover that I could often soothe their tears—and even get a few smiles—in less than one minute! It was a huge breakthrough.

"A mind once stretched to a new idea never returns to its original size."
—Oliver Wendell Holmes

Until recently, people mistakenly thought that most babies cried because of gassy stomach pain. Then, in my first book, *The Happiest Baby on the Block*, I offered a radical new idea: Essentially, our tiny babies are born three months before they're fully ready for the world. And when we create this "fourth trimester" for them by imitating the sensations they loved in the womb—the coziness, the sounds, and the rhythmic motions—they calm down much faster and sleep much longer.

Ah-ha! Suddenly, a lot of things made sense:

1. Car rides soothe fussing not by stopping gas pains, but by mimicking the motions and sounds within the womb and flipping on a baby's *calming reflex.*

2. Cuddling doesn't spoil babies, because before birth they're held 24/7! (So even holding a baby for twelve hours a day is a dramatic 50 percent cutback.)

3. Swaddling and strong white noise help babies sleep because they re-create the sensations they are familiar with from the womb.

4. Babies often cry when they're left unwrapped and alone in total quiet because of the sensory deprivation they experience—sort of like sticking an adult in a dark closet—which is such a contrast to the constant symphony of sensations they enjoyed in the womb.

Parents (and grandparents) who stretched their minds to the ideas in *The Happiest Baby* were quickly rewarded. Using my tips, they learned to soothe their babies' fussies *and* immediately add at least one to three hours to their infants' sleep!

Well, it turns out that you can be just as successful with toddler-calming and -cooperation as you can with baby-calming when you stretch your mind to the innovative key concept of *The Happiest Toddler:* Little kids are a lot like little cavemen.

Ah-ha! Suddenly, a lot of things make sense:

- Toddlers forget to say "please" and "thank you" because, like cavemen, they're impatient and impulsive. (They don't yet value these little niceties of society.)
- Toddlers bravely defy us, like cavemen hunting elephants and buffalo, even though we're many times their power and size!
- Toddlers, just like our ancient relatives, love face paint, sticking feathers in their hair, drawing on walls, and banging on drums.
- Toddlers have trouble being reasonable and rational (even on a good day) because, like early humans, their brains' language, logic, and patience control center is too immature.

But if the idea that toddlers are like cavemen sounds odd to you, don't take my word for it. Visit any park and watch the kids "at work." The five-year-olds act like little "people," taking turns and using words to settle conflicts, while the one-year-olds act like little "cavemen" (or even chimpanzees), walking clumsily, shoving to go first, and shrieking when upset.

Of course, even the wildest toddler isn't *really* a caveman! But you can use this concept like a magic window through which you can see your child's behavior in a profound new way.

And once you stretch your mind to accommodate this curious new idea and start learning the simple techniques in this book, you'll be stunned by how quickly your toddler's behavior will improve. You will literally be able to end 50 percent of tantrums in seconds *and* prevent 50 to 90 percent of outbursts before they even happen.

What if your toddler is the rare child who is sweet and mild and never has outbursts? Well, you'll find that *The Happiest Toddler* approach is *still* a great tool because it will help you:

- boost your child's patience, respect, and cooperation
- teach him to be a good friend and listener
- build his confidence and self-esteem
- help him to grow up emotionally happy and healthy

I know that sounds like a lot for one book to promise, but the tips you're about to learn really work! Which is why *The Happiest Toddler* quickly became the number one toddler book in America within weeks of its release in 2004.

So Why Did I Write a New Edition?

Since first writing *The Happiest Toddler*, I've spoken with thousands of parents, grandparents, educators, and health-care champions across the country. Their questions and feedback have helped me make the approach even easier to use.

This new, improved edition is loaded with new examples and illustrations. It's also more tightly organized and gets to the point faster, to help busy parents put the advice into action . . . immediately! Here's what you're about to learn:

Part One: Toddler/Parent Basics. The first part of the book discusses why toddlers behave the way they do and why that behavior can be so very, very hard on us. I'll discuss why your job is *not* to be the *boss* or *buddy* of your little child, but rather to be like an *ambassador*. (Ambassadors are diplomats who skillfully build great relationships by using respectful words and setting clear limits.)

Part Two: Toddler Communication Basics. Here you'll learn the two key skills that you need to become the best ambassador/parent on your block: the **Fast-Food Rule** (the key tip for connecting with *anyone* who is upset) and **Toddler-ese** (the easy way to translate anything you want to say into your toddler's natural language).

Part Three: Behavior Basics. In Part Three, you'll learn several highly effective ways to boost your child's good ("green-light") behaviors, curb annoying ("yellow-light") behaviors, and immediately stop unacceptable ("red-light") behaviors.

Part Four: How Do I Handle This One? Finally, I'll show you how to use *The Happiest Toddler* approach to quickly solve everyday challenges such as tantrums, fears, defiance, dawdling, biting, picky eating, and many more.

In this book, you will pick up many highly effective parenting tips . . . some that even lead to instant improvement! Pick a few that make the most sense to you and—here's the important part—try to practice them several times a day for a week or two. Practice is the key. Through practice you will build your (and your child's) confidence and success. And bit by bit, as you feel more competent and effective, you and your child will develop a relationship that is full of fun, respect, and caring.

Now I'm thrilled to invite you to read on and learn how to help *your* wonderful little child become the *happiest toddler on the block.*

Note: I recommend that you begin using the approach described in this book when your child is around nine months of age. Starting when your child is very young will help you avoid many problems *before* they occur. But even if you begin years later, I promise you'll find that *The Happiest Toddler* approach will help you every single day—well past your child's fourth birthday. In fact, parents often comment that these skills have improved their connection with their older children, their bosses, their neighbors . . . and even with their *own* parents.

The
Happiest Toddler
on the Block

PART ONE

The Happiest Toddler

Toddler/Parent Basics

What makes your toddler tick? And what is it about your toddler's behavior that makes you swing between feeling tickled . . . and ticked off?

♦ **Chapter 1** is a speed course on the daily challenges that toddlers have to handle. This information is designed to help you better understand why young tots do some of the crazy things that drive you wild.

♦ **Chapter 2** looks at parenting from *your* side of the high chair. There are good reasons why caring for toddlers is such tough work. I will teach you why the most successful parents think of themselves as *ambassadors* to these primitive little people.

1

Toddler Basics:
The Gentle Art of
Civilizing a Toddler

"A two-year-old is kind of like having a blender, but you don't have a top for it."

—Jerry Seinfeld

Main Points:

- Toddlers aren't mini-adults, or even mini–big kids. They're more like uncivilized little *cave-kids*.

- Our homes tend to be either too boring or too stimulating for our toddlers.

- Your tot's brain struggles with language and logic . . . *especially* when he's upset.

- Your toddler's normal developmental drives often put him on a direct collision course with you.

- You'll find parenting makes a lot more sense once you figure out your child's unique . . . temperament.

Would you like to help your child become the best, most co-operative toddler on your block? You'll be most successful if you keep in mind this one key fact: Toddlers act less like little schoolkids than they do like uncivilized little . . . cavemen.

Wait a minute, you might be thinking. *Did he just compare my child to a caveman?* Yup, I did!

Of course, toddlers aren't really cavemen, but they *do* exhibit lots of pretty primitive behaviors, like grunting and pointing, wiping their noses on their sleeves (or yours), scratching and biting when angry, and peeing anywhere they want. No wonder the mom of a headstrong 18-month-old jokingly told me, "It's like there's a tiny *Neanderthal* living in my house!"

In fact, between your child's first and fourth birthdays, his rapid maturation will greatly resemble a superfast rerun of ancient human development. It's thrilling to watch as the same great achievements that took our primitive ancestors eons to master spring forth in our children over the space of just three years:

- walking upright
- the ability to skillfully use the hands and fingers
- talking
- juggling ideas (comparing/contrasting)
- beginning to read

One of your biggest challenges during these years will be to teach your child the finer points of "civilization," such as manners, patience, and concern for others. But I promise that you will be much less frustrated and much more successful teaching these good behaviors once you recognize

that your uncivilized little friend is far from a fully rational and logical person.

The Little Adult Assumption

To soothe a toddler who is having a blowup, many parents are taught to calmly acknowledge their child's unhappy feelings and then gently correct them: "Jane, I know you want the ball, but it's Billy's turn. Remember we talked about sharing? So please give the ball back to Billy. You can have the next turn. Okay?"

Sounds reasonable, but mature comments like those often backfire and can make livid toddlers shriek even louder! That's because little children aren't mini-adults. Their immature toddler brains struggle to understand long sentences and to control their bursts of powerful emotions.

Psychologist Thomas Phelan, author of *1-2-3 Magic,* calls our attempt to use calm logic to soothe upset toddlers "the little adult assumption." By that he means we are expecting stressed-out toddlers to settle down because of our explanations and our polite appeals to reason—which is simply unrealistic. Too many parents believe their little ones should be able to turn off their emotions mid-tantrum and maturely reply, "Thank you for explaining that, Mother. I'll happily do what you want." Hmmm . . . I don't think so!

You'll be far more successful calming your upset tyke and getting his cooperation if you replace adult-style statements with the simple, basic phrases you'll learn in Chapters 3 and 4. And believe me, you'll have plenty of opportunity to practice this special approach over the next few years, because even sweet, happy toddlers have emotional upsets several times a day.

Why are toddlers so prone to outbursts? There are many reasons, but here are the top four. . . .

Your Toddler's Four Big Struggles

We all know how tough it is to raise and civilize a toddler, but have you ever stopped to think how tough it is to BE a toddler?

From your toddler's perspective, she is losing *all day long*! She's weaker, slower, and shorter than everyone else . . . and that's just the start of her challenges. Toddlers face four big struggles every day that make it extra-hard for them to behave like little angels.

- Our modern world is weird to them.
- Their brains are out of balance.
- Their normal development can make them misbehave.
- Their temperaments can make them overreact.

Toddler Struggle #1: Our Modern World Is Weird to Them.

We assume that living in a house or apartment is normal, but it's actually a very weird environment for toddlers. That's because for 99.9 percent of human history, children spent most of every day frolicking . . . outside.

Imagine inviting Tarzan to live with you. There's a good chance he'd go totally bonkers. Compared to his jungle home, yours delivers an unpleasant double whammy: terribly dull in some ways, yet way too exciting in other ways.

Similarly, our homes are both boring *and* overstimulating to our little kids . . . at the same time. They're boring because they replace the exciting sensations of nature (the bright colors, the feeling of the wind on their skin, the brilliant sun, the soft grass, etc.) with an immense stillness (flat walls, flat floors, no wind, no fluttering shadows, no birds chirping). Additionally, many traditional toddlers' delights (running after kids and dogs, throwing dirt clods, catching bugs, climbing trees) are literally beyond reach.

When you think of it that way, it's no wonder so many kids are bouncing off the walls by late morning.

Yet, at the same time our modern world can be too stimulating to toddlers. It bombards them with jolting experiences that kids in the past never had to deal with: crazy cartoons, slick videos, clanging computer games, noisy toys, and bright colors everywhere. We may be used to all this, but it can make many little children feel stressed.

As the day wears on, all this *over*- and *under*stimulation can drive many little kids over the edge into fatigue, irritation, and misbehavior. Uh-oh! *Tilt . . . tilt . . . tilt!*

Toddler Struggle #2: Their Brains Are Out of Balance.

Your toddler's brain is like a buzzing beehive with twenty billion cells and 50 percent more nerve connections than we have in our big heads! All these connections mean millions—

or billions—of signals zipping around. "Go here!" "Go there!" "Touch it!" "No, don't!" Yikes! No wonder little kids spin out of control.

To help manage this whirlwind of mental activity, our brains are split into a right half and a left. The two halves of the brain look alike but do very different things. The left half is the methodical *nerd* of the nervous system. It loves details: picking the right word, counting the toys, and solving problems . . . step by step. It helps us listen carefully, be logical, and stay calm.

The right half is the hyper "Speedy Gonzales" of the nervous system. It's great at quick decisions, instant face recognition, and bouncing to the beat of any type of music. Unlike the thoughtful left side, the right side is distractible, impulsive, and emotional.

The two halves of the brain are in pretty close balance in big kids and adults, but the left side tends to be a bit more in control. Guess which half runs the show in toddlers? Yup, you guessed it . . . the right. In fact, your tot's emotional right side is so busy and noisy it often ignores the patient voice of the left side telling it to settle down.

And as if all that weren't challenging enough, your toddler's brain gets thrown even more off balance when she's upset. Big emotions instantly *shut down* the thoughtful left brain and dramatically *amp up* the primitive right.

In truth, this same imbalance occurs in adults, too (that's why we "go ape" when we're upset). But since toddlers are a whole lot more impulsive to begin with, our little friends shriek, spit, crash into tables, run into streets, and act even more like Neanderthals than usual when they get upset.

Despite these difficulties, your toddler's right brain has one absolutely spectacular ability that will become one of your best tools for connecting with her and civilizing and

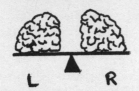

NORMAL ADULT
(calm, logical)

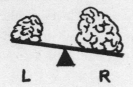

NORMAL TODDLER
(impulsive, distractable)

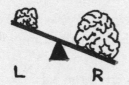

UPSET TODDLER
(wild, rude)

calming her, too: the capacity to respond to "nonverbal" communication. Even when her immature left brain gets hopelessly confused by your *words,* her right brain will have no problem understanding your tone of voice, the look on your face, and your gestures . . . even when she's upset.

You don't need to become a brain expert, but knowing a bit of science will help you understand one very important point: Talking directly to the right brain when your child is upset, by using your tone of voice, gestures, and body language to mirror a bit of her emotion, is the key to helping her calm back down. You'll become an expert at this method when you learn the Fast-Food Rule and Toddler-ese in Chapter 3.

By the end of your child's toddler years, you'll easily be able to see her "new and improved" left brain taking more control. This will help her be more verbal, more focused, and less likely to pop like a firecracker at every little frustration.

Sign Language: Young Kids Know More Than They Can Say

When you think about it, it's not so easy to talk. Like a marching band, your lips, tongue, and throat have to move together with perfect split-second teamwork.

It takes most kids two to three years to get really good at speaking, but a fun way to jump-start your one-year-old's ability to "talk" is to teach her to sign. Remember, your toddler's right brain is an expert at reading gestures. That's why even very young toddlers can learn sign language.

> *Jane noticed that her 15-month-old son raised his hands whenever he wanted to leave. So she started to use this sign to "tell" him when it was time to go.*

There are many good books that help parents teach their children sign language. Or you can just make up your own signs. Here are a few easy ones you'll have fun with. Say the word out loud as you show your child the gesture.

- Put your hand to your mouth for "eat."
- Suck on your fist for "drink."
- Stroke the back of your hand for "doggie."
- Wiggle your finger for "worm."
- Sniff to mean "flower."
- Pat the top of your head for "hat."
- Repeatedly open, then clench your hand for "breast-feed."

Four-year-olds are definitely more patient, more civilized, and well on their way to growing up.

(Want to read more about how your child's brain works? I recommend taking a look at these two great books: *What's Going On in There?*, by Lise Eliot, and *The Scientist in the Crib*, by Alison Gopnick, Andrew Meltzoff, and Patricia Kuhl.)

Toddler Struggle #3: Their Normal Development Can Make Them Misbehave.

Believe it or not, toddlers are biologically driven to do many of the things that drive us bonkers. Let's focus on a few of the developmental characteristics typical of all toddlers, and likely to put them on a collision course with their parents:

- **Toddlers are compulsive walkers . . . and climbers.** After months of being limited to lying down, sitting, and crawling, suddenly being able to walk and climb is absolutely thrilling. Your primitive little friend will roam around nonstop from dawn to dusk, feeling *Wow, this is soooo cool!*
- **Toddlers are very self-centered.** Most toddlers demand to be in the spotlight: *Talk about me!* It's a wonder their first word is usually "ma ma" . . . and not "me me"!
- **Toddlers have trouble switching gears.** Little tots often have trouble going from one activity to the next. They seem like machines without an "off" switch. You see this all the time in their play: *Whee! Let's whack this drum . . .* a thousand times *in a row!*
- **Toddlers have the attention span of a bumblebee.** Young kids flit from thing to thing. Their high degree of distractibility is perfectly illustrated in the following diagram, from Louise Bates Ames and Francis Ilg's wonderful book, *Your One-Year-Old.* As toddlers mature, they gradually become able to focus their concentration for longer periods of time.
- **Toddlers are rigid.** Two-year-olds are *not* famous for flexibility. You can see this even in the way young toddlers approach the rules of language. For

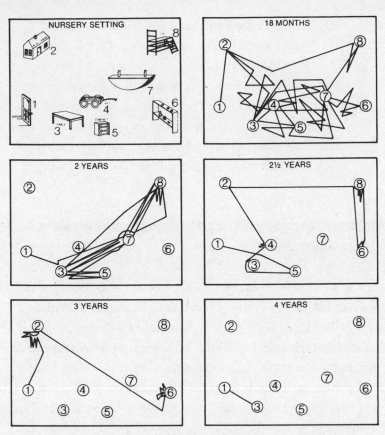

Seven Clocked Minutes of Nursery School Behavior at Different Ages

example, once they learn that adding "s" makes things plural, they may say "foots" instead of "feet," and are likely to continue doing so no matter how many times you correct them. The same is true for their lack of flexibility about any changes that occur in their daily lives. For example, your tot may get really upset if one night you deviate from your normal routine and forget to say "Sweet dreams!" to her dollies. And like us, the more stressed and tired they feel, the more rigid they become.

- **Toddlers can't stop pushing the limits.** A *parent's* job is to set smart limits, and a *toddler's* job is to *push* those limits. Toddlers literally can't stop themselves from exploring, touching, and pulling on everything. That's how they learn about the world and about themselves. So while *you* may feel that your little friend keeps defying you, *she* may feel you're unfairly blocking her greatest joy—discovery.

Toddler Struggle #4: Their Temperaments Can Make Them Overreact.

Every toddler is a totally unique person with his very own face and voice . . . even his personality is one-of-a-kind.

Each child is born with a personality as matchless as his fingerprints. It's a mixture of intelligence, humor, and a fascinating quality called *temperament.*

His temperament is his style of interacting with the world: his pacing, attitude, flexibility, and general mood. Is he cautious or brave? Stubborn or easygoing? Mild or passionate? Temperament explains why some of us can sleep with the TV on while others go nuts with the tiniest noise, why some forgive easily and others just can't let go. Knowing your child's temperament helps you know when to pamper and when to push.

Temperament tends to pass from parent to child. So, shy parents often have shy kids and passionate parents usually have little chili peppers. But sometimes nature throws a curveball and a couple of librarians beget a heavy-metal rocker!

Knowing your child's *developmental stage* tells you what milestone he's approaching, but knowing his *temperament*

lets you predict whether he'll greet it with gusto or approach it with caution.

So what temperament does your child have? Is he a calm little Buddha or Attila the Hun? In general, temperament comes in one of three categories: easy, shy, and spirited. While some kids fall between these categories, about three out of every four are easy to peg.

Easy temperament

Evan, 26 months old, wakes up in a good mood and wanders into the kitchen for breakfast. But a potential crisis occurs when his favorite cereal is

*"gone-gone" after only a few flakes have been
poured into the bowl. His dad, Chuck, quickly
takes another brand of cereal from the pantry
and sprinkles it into the bowl. "Mmm!" Chuck
urges. "Your other favorite! Ohmygod it's
yummy! Try it!" Evan plunges his spoon into the
milk—and finishes the whole bowl!*

About half of all kids are easygoing. They wake up "on the
right side of the bed," cheerful and ready for a new day.
They're active (but not wild), tolerate changes well, and enjoy
new people and situations.

Easy kids are resilient. They bounce back from bangs and
disappointments with a smile. Yet when push comes to shove,
they're perfectly capable of both pushing and shoving!

Shy temperament

*Eighteen-month-old Jesse was a cautious guy.
His mom, Jody, said, "He only speaks four words,
but he's a thinker. He practices things in his mind
before he does them." At the park, he spent
weeks carefully watching kids crawl through a
little tunnel. Then one day he tried it himself.
After he made his way through, he was so giddy
that he did it twenty times in a row.*

About 15 percent of kids are shy, cautious, and slow to
warm up to new experiences. By nine months most easy babies smile at strangers passing by, but shy kids frown and cling
to us for safety, frequently waving bye-bye only *after* a guest
leaves. Cautious kids are often extra-sensitive. They don't like
their milk too cold or pants that are too scratchy. They're easily frustrated, fearful, and clingy, often trailing us from room
to room, and unhappy with changes. Cautious kids also tend

to be very observant. These are the kids who recognize where they're going and may start to cry a block before you even arrive at the doctor's office! They are often early talkers but late walkers, and their motto is "When in doubt . . . don't!"

Your shy tot may start the "terrible twos" early (15 to 18 months), but if you treat him with patience and respect he will finish the toddler years happy and confident. (*Warning:* Shy, cautious young children should be shielded from pressure and excessive criticism. That type of rejection can make a shy child fearful and rigid for the rest of his life.)

Spirited temperament

> Fifteen-month-old Gina stays busy from dawn till dark, flying from one activity to another. "If she can't open a door, she knocks it down!" says her mom. When she's moving, she's happy. But her constant activity means she forever needs boo-boos kissed, trips to the park, and parents who are vigilant about childproofing the house.

One in ten toddlers is a strong-willed, spirited tyke. These "roller-coaster kids" have high highs and low lows. And when the sparks of daily stress mix with the TNT of their explosive personalities . . . *KABOOM!*

Parents usually know if they have a spirited/challenging child, because they're the "more" kids:

- more active (they run farther, jump higher, and spin longer)
- more impatient (they hate sharing and taking turns)
- more impulsive (they're easily distracted and accident-prone)
- more defiant (they run to the curb, look back at you . . . then dash into the street)

- more rigid (they get so upset, they keep crying even *after* getting what they want)
- more intense (they get *very* glad, *very* sad, and *very* mad)
- more sensitive (their feelings are easily hurt)

These superactive kids range from cheery to moody, stubborn, and defiant. Fortunately, spirited children usually grow into happy, enthusiastic kids as long as they get lots of outside play, consistent but flexible limits, and a steady supply of patience and love.

Temperament: Easy, Shy, or Spirited

Let's take your toddler's temperament "temperature." Look over these nine traits and circle the words that best fit your child.

	Easy	**Shy**	**Spirited**
Activity	Active	Likes quiet play	Fidgets a lot and is very active
Regularity	Predictable eating, sleeping	Predictable eating, sleeping	Unpredictable patterns
First reaction to new people	Interest	Reluctance	Either delight or rejection
Handles unexpected change	Easily	Reluctantly or unhappily	Easily, or gets very upset

	Easy	Shy	Spirited
Intensity of feelings	Mild/gentle	May be mild or spirited	Spirited/ passionate
Usual mood	Happy/ easygoing	Happy but easily thrown off balance	Big ups and downs
Persistence	Okay with not getting his way	May give up or be tenacious	Doesn't give up
Distractibility	Focused	Very focused	Easily distracted
Sensitive to noises/smells	Not much	Ultrasensitive	Not much, or a lot

Variety *Is* the Spice of Life (and the Foundation of Society!)

It would be terrible if there were no doctors in the world, but it would also be terrible if everyone were a doctor. We need leaders and followers, thinkers and doers, worriers and risk-takers. Different temperaments help fill all the niches of society.

So although you may unexpectedly find yourself with the tough job of raising a *saber-toothed tiger,* remember that some day your little tiger will have an important role to play in the world.

The Ten-Second Temperament Test

Still not sure which category describes your child? This little test may help: Go to an uncrowded mall, release your child's hand, and pretend to turn your back for two seconds. (Keep a close watch out of the corner of your eye.) What does she do? Stand there? (Easy.) Grab your coat and cry? (Shy.) Run away without looking back? (Spirited.) The answer will give you a pretty good reading of your child's temperament.

Now that you have a better sense what makes your little friend tick, and what may be preventing her from behaving the way you want her to, let's explore the special struggles that the parents of toddlers face every day.

2

Parenting Basics:
The Lowdown on Bringing Up a Toddler

"There are times when parenthood seems like nothing more than feeding the hand that bites you."

—Peter De Vries

Main Points:

- *No one* was meant to parent a toddler . . . without a lot of help.

- Toddlers are tricky even for experienced parents.

- Your tot's words or deeds may open up feelings of hurt and humiliation from deep in your past.

- Young kids are especially hard to deal with if their temperaments clash with ours.

- The key to effective parenting: Be an "ambassador"! The best parents diplomatically mix sincere respect and clear limits.

Parenting is the greatest joy—and the toughest job. You love your child, but . . . *oooff!* One minute your tot is the apple of your eye, the next she's the pebble in your shoe.

Every mom and dad I've ever met has confronted some or all of the following four struggles that can make the toddler years even more challenging:

 Parents' Four Big Struggles

- We don't get enough help and guidance.
- Daily battles can make us feel like failures.
- Our toddlers' actions can "push our buttons."
- Our temperaments may clash with our children's.

Parent Struggle #1: We Don't Get Enough Help and Guidance

> *"It takes a village to raise a child."*
>
> —African proverb

Man, it's hard spending a whole day entertaining a young child. How did our grandparents do it? The truth is . . . they didn't.

The whole idea of the nuclear family (a household of just parents and kids) is a recent invention. In fact, it's one of the biggest experiments in human history. Our ancestors always lived in *extended* families (near grandparents, aunts, cousins, etc.).

For thousands of years, parents had the village to help them. In fact, when people from more traditional cultures hear about our spread-out families, they're usually stunned. "You can't be serious!" they say. "How can you raise a baby without your sisters, mother, aunts, and friends?"

More and more, we leave our hometowns, have fewer older children to help out, don't know the neighbors, and live in single-parent families or families where both parents work full-time jobs.

Sure, we have lots of modern conveniences (like cars and washing machines), but they can never make up for the loss of family, neighbors, and community. No wonder parents feel overwhelmed. We are! And when you add to that some other modern trends like drive-through restaurants, online shopping, e-mail, and telecommuting, it's plain to see that we live in little worlds that are increasingly isolated from one another.

What is the result of these changes? Amazingly, today's parents often work longer hours than most parents in past generations. That's because they either have to supervise their kids 24/7 without help or spend all day at work and then come home to a house full of undone chores.

The challenge of parenting is especially great today because, unlike parents in earlier generations who often cared for younger siblings or babysat the neighbor's children, most of us have little to no experience raising kids. We get training for our jobs, and we take driver's ed, but when it comes to parenthood, we're supposed to just figure it out on our own.

So please, give yourself a round of applause. You're not a wimp if you use a babysitter or a housecleaner. You're not selfish if you get away for lunch with a friend or take an exercise class. Too many parents undermine themselves with guilt. Give yourself credit for all the good work you're doing . . . and get yourself some help.

Finding Your Village

Whether you live in Manhattan, New York, or Manhattan, Kansas, you can find, or create, communities of child-rearing support all around you:

- Set up playdates with a friend who has a toddler the same age as yours.
- Get to know your neighbors.
- Enroll your child in nursery school or preschool, a Mother's Day Out program, or Mommy and Me–type playgroups. (Age two is not too young.)
- Join a gym or activity group targeted to parents and toddlers.
- Join a playgroup or babysitting co-op. (Check your pediatrician's bulletin board or a community newspaper or Web site.)
- Look for online communities for moms of toddlers.
- Invite an older neighbor to visit with your child.
- Join a place of worship.
- Move nearer to your family or move them nearer to you.

Parent Struggle #2: Daily Battles Can Make Us Feel Like Failures

"Perfection is only found in the dictionary."

—Old saying

Lynne was in tears. That morning her 20-month-old, Josh, sank his teeth into a child at playgroup. It was the third time this week he had bitten someone, and this time he did it so hard the teacher asked Lynne not to bring Josh back. She sobbed, "What am I doing wrong?"

We proudly take credit when our kids behave well, so it is only natural for us to feel responsible when they misbehave. But before you rush to judge yourself, remember that toddler limit-pushing is totally normal. Whether you're a CEO or a four-star general, your toddler is going to break the rules.

We all mess up sometimes, but failing every now and then doesn't make us failures; it's a normal part of parenting and can actually speed us along the path to success. So relax and learn to look at your mistakes with a sense of humor. Believe it or not, these toddler years will be gone in a flash, and one day you'll miss them terribly. Take a big breath, and know that your love, respect, and guidance will help you finish these years with a happy, confident, likable child at your side!

Here's one more bit of consolation for you: Toddlers save their biggest meltdowns for their parents. We're the people

---

Bad Day? You're in Good Company!

"If at first you don't succeed, you're running about average."

—M. H. Anderson

Even the greatest geniuses fail . . . many, many times! Dr. Seuss, America's beloved children's author, was rejected twenty-eight times before he found a publisher for *The Cat in the Hat*. Barbra Streisand's off-Broadway debut opened and closed the same night. Walt Disney was once fired because he "lacked imagination" and "had no original ideas."

Luckily, parenthood is chock-full of second chances. So if you're having a tough day, don't get stuck obsessing over it. To paraphrase Scarlett O'Hara in *Gone With the Wind*, tomorrow really is another day.

with whom they feel the safest. So you might consider your primitive little friend's tantrums a form of flattery.

Parent Struggle #3: Our Toddlers' Actions Can "Push Our Buttons"

"There are days when everything my boy does pushes my buttons. I end up feeling like I'm one big button!"

—Peter, dad of three-year-old Andrew

Toddlers do have a way of pushing our buttons. Their actions can unleash from within us strong, often irrational *over-reactions*. Sometimes we get so angry we literally can't think straight or control what we say. And, the more stressed we get, the more *we* start acting like primitives ourselves.

What's the biggest reason we lose it with our toddlers? Their behavior triggers *demons* from our past.

Here's what I mean: Our kids' actions may release sudden waves of memory. Sometimes these can be wonderful. For example, watching your child lick the bowl may bring back a happy memory of you making cookies with your mom. But other times they can be deeply upsetting. Fragments of painful past experiences dwell inside us all, waiting for a catalyst to bring them to the surface again. For example, being slapped in the face by your two-year-old may suddenly rekindle the anger you felt when you were slapped by your father (or, more recently, when you were insulted by a boss). If your child laughs when you accidentally spill soup down your shirt, that might bring back the deep hurt you felt when you were taunted by schoolmates or mocked by a sarcastic grandmother.

Often we react without any specific memory of a similar situation. But if you feel a sudden surge of anger, hurt, or resentment, that's a pretty sure sign that your child's action has tapped into some strongly upsetting early experience.

Making peace with your past

Debby was proud to go out to dinner for Mother's Day with her husband, Andy, and their three-year-old twins, Sophie and Audrey. But her happiness turned to hurt when the girls started fighting over who would sit next to Andy: "I don't want Mommy! I want Daddy!" She unexpectedly felt the sting of rejection she remembered from when she was a child and kids on the playground wouldn't let her join in to play any of their games.

Remember, when we get mad or hurt, our rational left brain shuts down and the emotional right side takes over. That's why, in the heat of the moment, it's easy to forget that your toddler isn't intentionally trying to hurt or humiliate you. Your tot's spitting, scratching, and defiance are just the primitive acts of an immature, uncivilized little person who has trouble controlling herself, and hasn't learned to anticipate—or care—how others feel.

A better response when your buttons get pushed

Sara Jane said, "The other day, I got so mad I threw the remote control and broke it. I had angry parents, and I'm so afraid of losing my temper with Kimmie. But something inside me just snaps when she looks right at me and disobeys. It's like she's daring me to do something!"

No parent *wants* to scream at her toddler, but sometimes anger just erupts out of nowhere. I don't want you to ignore your feelings, but it is simply not okay to explode in front of your child. Your child can't help acting like a caveman, but you can . . . and must. It's your responsibility to do your *utmost* never to lash out with physical violence or hurtful words.

Take a breath . . . forgive yourself (we all have old pains that make us overreact) . . . and try to understand why you got so upset. Review the outburst in your mind or write it down in a journal. Anger may be the initial reaction to your child's misbehavior, but anger is usually just a shell that covers our deeper feelings, like fear, hurt, shame, or betrayal.

Try to find the hurt that's *under* your anger. Your daughter's words or actions might have made you mad, but she is not the one who hurt you in the past. Can you recall an early experience that triggered similar feelings? Remembering will allow you to use your adult ability to analyze these feelings and put them in proper perspective.

Once you realize which feelings lie *beneath* your anger, spend a minute to realize how unfair it was for you to have been treated in that way when you were a child. But you will be a happier person, and a better parent, if you can forgive those who caused you pain. Make your peace . . . let go of the past . . . savor the present.

Those are the first healthy steps to parenting thoughtfully instead of reactively.

So what should you do when your toddler does something that makes your blood boil? Here are a few options:

- Scowl, clap your hands hard a few times, and make a rumbly growl. Then, sternly say, "No!" (See page 176 for more about this supereffective tactic.)

- Turn away for thirty seconds and take some deep breaths (see **magic breathing,** page 125).
- Put your child in a safe place, then go punch the mattress or scream into a pillow.

And if you find yourself getting flaming mad over and over again, here are some smart strategies to help you keep your cool:

- Talk about your painful feelings and memories with someone you trust.
- Get more help at home or put your tot in preschool.
- Don't spread yourself thin. Look for ways you can lighten your load a little.
- Plan some fun little treats every day (even if it's just a ten-minute break for reading a magazine).
- Get more sleep.
- Ask your doctor or spiritual counselor about support groups and other resources.

And if you do lose your temper with your child, use it as an opportunity to "turn lemons into lemonade." Apologize as soon as you cool down. Then, later in the day, take a moment to calmly talk about how you wish you and she had behaved, and remind her that you'll have plenty of chances to practice getting it right and that your love is *way* stronger than anger.

"Bedtime Sweet Talk"

Many of us take our daily accomplishments for granted, yet beat ourselves up over our mistakes. However, just as we praise our kids for their **baby steps** of progress, we need to do the same for our own baby steps of success. Here's a simple way to boost your optimism, resilience, and happiness that's almost like saying nightly prayers. I call it **bedtime sweet talk.**

Each night at bedtime, remind yourself of two or three of the tiny successes or happy experiences from the day that has just passed: "I had many blessings today, like meeting the new neighbor down the street; dinner came out great; I didn't yell at my child even once."

Take sixty seconds to jot these down in a notebook. I guarantee they'll bring a smile to your face every time you look back at them . . . for many years to come.

The amazing thing about bedtime sweet talk is that pretty soon you'll start noticing how much more is going *right* in your life than you thought. (Read more about using bedtime sweet talk with your toddler on page 129.)

Parent Struggle #4: Our Temperaments May Clash with Our Children's

> Is your child a chip off the old block—or a mutant from Mars? Are the two of you peas in a pod . . . or sparks and dynamite?

In the last chapter, I discussed the large contribution your toddler's inborn temperament makes to her behavior. Now let's turn the tables and look at *your* temperament. (Yes, you have one too!)

> Judy was a "60 mph" kind of woman, but her kids were slow as molasses. In fact, Judy nicknamed Emily and Ted "Speed Bump #1" and "Speed Bump #2" because they forced her to switch from her normal fast pace to a turtle's creep.

Few of us mesh perfectly with our children. Psychologists have a term for how well a parent's temperament matches up with his child's: *goodness of fit.* And, unlike with lovers, opposites don't always attract.

Do any of the following describe how you match up with your toddler?

I'm neat and disciplined.	My daughter is a little Pigpen.
I love to cuddle.	My son pushes me away when I hug him.
I'm athletic.	My son is low energy and would rather read.
I'm the life of the party.	My son is timid and cries around strangers.
I'm soft-spoken.	My daughter is opinionated, defiant, and wild.

We usually have the easiest time getting along with children who are similar to us. But not always. For example, stubborn parents with stubborn kids can be an explosive mix.

What's Your Fit? Check out the list of temperament traits on pages 20–21. See how you rate on qualities like intensity, mood, and so forth. How do you compare with your toddler? Where do you complement each other and where do you collide? Half the challenge in parenting (and all close personal relationships) is being able to manage your personality differences.

Are You Your Toddler's Boss or Buddy?

During infancy, we happily give our babies everything they want: milk, a clean diaper, cozy cuddling. We bend over backward and savor the sweet reward of their laughter and hugs.

Then, around the first birthday, something changes. Our child starts crawling, walking, and screaming out her strong opinions ("Gimme!!!"). We will still try to be "reasonable" and give 90 percent of what she wants, but 10 percent of the time we just can't or don't want to bend to our child's request. And guess what? She's not going to like that.

We lovingly acknowledge her feelings. She throws a fit!

We use reason. She throws a fit!

We distract . . . we explain . . . we warn. She throws a fit!

Pretty soon *we're* having a fit too. And the two of us are going at it like a couple of pro wrestlers.

So what *are* you supposed to do?

At my lectures, bewildered parents often ask what to do to get their kids to behave: "Should I be more lenient? More tough? Am I breaking her spirit? Giving in too much?" They're confused about teaching obedience because they don't have a lot of personal experience and they're bombarded with contradictory advice: Be giving! Be strict! Be a friend! Be the boss!

Most of us want to respond to our children's demands with kindness and generosity, hoping that they will follow our lead and learn to be kind in return. But unfortunately, trying to be a "buddy" and repeatedly giving in to your primitive little friend's demands may end up teaching her that whining works and turn her into a spoiled brat.

On the other hand, all parents are warned to back up their rules with swift, predictable consequences if they want to raise an obedient child and keep order in their home. But if that really worked, parenting would be a snap. You'd just command your child to stop . . . and she would. Unfortunately, parents who try to be their child's "boss" rely too much on threats and often end up *inflaming* confrontations rather than reducing them (especially with strong-willed, tenacious tots).

So what's a parent supposed to do?

Be an Ambassador to Your Toddler

The truth is we don't live in a black-and-white world. Sometimes you'll act like your child's buddy and sometimes her boss, but the best way to understand your job is to think of yourself as an *ambassador* . . . an ambassador from the 21st century to the "uncivilized" little munchkin living in your home.

I know what you're probably thinking: *Ambassador? What the heck does he mean?*

Well, you know what ambassadors do, right? They go to foreign countries and build good relations by giving, giving, giving. They give aid, throw parties, and show respect. But they're not pushovers. When there's a serious conflict, they put their foot down: *"My country will not tolerate this."*

As parental "ambassadors" we do the exact same thing. We build good relations with our kids by giving, giving, giving. We give food, love, toys, backrubs—we're forever giving. But from time to time we also need to put our foot down, set a firm limit and enforce it.

To build good relationships with dukes and kings, the world's best ambassadors all must master two key skills:

- communicating with respect (to avoid ruining the relationship by accidentally offending their host)
- speaking the language of the country they're visiting (Even the best ambassador will fail if she can't speak the language of the people with whom she's working.)

Similarly, to build good relationships with their tots, the world's best parents must master the same key diplomatic skills:

- communicating with respect
- speaking the language a toddler's immature brain can understand

In the next section, you'll have some fun mastering these two powerful parenting skills.

PART TWO

Connect with Respect:

Toddler Communication

Basics

In Part One, I discussed why it helps to think of a young child's mind as "uncivilized" and why toddlers are such a challenge for today's parents. Now, in Part Two, I want to teach you two of the most important parenting skills you'll ever learn.

♦ **Chapter 3** will give you an extraordinarily simple way to communicate respectfully with anyone (especially someone who's upset): the Fast-Food Rule.

♦ **Chapter 4** will tell you how to translate your caring, respectful words into your tot's "native tongue," a very simple language I call Toddler-ese.

Within days, these two skills will bring about a huge jump in your tot's cooperation and a huge drop in tantrums. Best of all, by using the Fast-Food Rule and Toddler-ese every day you will boost your child's health and happiness and set him on the path of kindness and confidence for the rest of his life.

The "Fast-Food Rule":
The Golden Rule of Communication

"When people talk, listen completely. Most people never listen."

—Ernest Hemingway

Main Points:

- The secret to communicating with anybody who's upset is the Fast-Food Rule (FFR).

- FFR Part 1: Whoever is most upset talks first; the other person listens, repeats back what they're told, and only then do they take their turn to talk.

- FFR Part 2: What you say to an upset person is not as important as the way you say it (this is what I call finding the "sweet spot").

- The best parents use the FFR instead of words that hurt, compare, distract, and rush to squelch feelings.

You smile, then your baby smiles, then you smile back. She babbles, you babble, then she gurgles with glee. This little "dance" is your child's first conversation. The simple back-and-forth of patiently listening . . . then responding is the basic turn-taking pattern of *all* human communication.

This little dance is simple and automatic when your toddler is happy. But when he enters *meltdown* mode it's easy for you to get sucked in, lose your cool, and start to melt down, too (especially when *you* are the target of the outburst). This dynamic can lead to an explosive escalation.

But don't worry! This is exactly when the Fast-Food Rule comes to the rescue.

 ## The What? The *Fast-Food Rule*!

This silly-sounding rule is the golden rule for communicating with anyone who's upset. I promise: You'll be amazed how it works on *everyone*—from toddlers to teens to temperamental spouses.

In a nutshell, the Fast-Food Rule says: Whenever you talk to someone who's upset, always repeat *his* feelings first . . . *before* offering your own comments or advice.

Why Is This Called the Fast-Food Rule?

Fast-food joints may have their problems, but they do one thing incredibly well: communicating with customers.

Imagine you're hungry. You pull up to the restaurant order window and a voice crackles over the speaker, "Can I help you?" You answer, "A burger and fries, please."

Now . . . tell me what do you think the order-taker will say back to you?

- "What's the matter, too lazy to cook tonight?"
- "You should get two burgers, you look hungry."
- "That's five dollars, please drive forward."

The answer is *none of the above*!

The very first thing she will do is *repeat your order* to you. She does this because she needs to make sure she understands exactly what you want ("Okay, that's a burger and fries. Anything to drink?") before she takes *her* turn: "That's five dollars. Please drive up front."

I mentioned at the start of this chapter that normal conversations have a simple back-and-forth pattern. When we talk, we take turns ("I like chocolate!" "Me too! I *love* chocolate!").

But this pattern changes dramatically when one person is upset.

The rule for talking to someone who's upset is: Whoever is most upset *talks first* (and gets an extralong turn to vent). The other person listens patiently and repeats back his feelings with care and interest ("Wow! What she did really made you angry!"). Only then does the friend get a turn to say what *she* thinks about the situation.

At fast-food joints, the person who is hungriest gets to speak first. And with parents and children (or in any dialogue between two people), the person who is most upset—the "hungriest for attention"—goes first. This is Part 1 of the Fast-Food Rule.

Is it really so important to take turns like this? Absolutely! Here's why: Agitated people are *terrible* listeners. Big emotions (like anger and fear) turn our open minds into closed doors. But once we express our feelings—and they're acknowledged—our minds swing back open and we can again pay attention to the good suggestions of the people we love.

And There Is One More Critical Point

When you repeat what a person has shared with you about her feelings, *what you say* (your words) is not as important as *the way you say it* (your tone of voice, facial expression, and gestures). This is Part 2 of the Fast-Food Rule.

Many Moms and Dads say that the Fast-Food Rule is one of the most important parenting (and life) skills they've ever learned. So now let's see how to use both parts of the FFR (the words you say *and* the way you say them) in some real-life situations.

FFR Part 1: Restate the Upset Person's Feelings

Imagine that a woman is frantic because she lost a folder of documents she needs for work. Weeping, she calls her mother: "Mom, I feel so stupid! I left some very important papers on my seat at a restaurant! My boss is going to kill me!"

Immediately the mother interrupts. "It's okay, sweetheart. I'm sure he'll understand. Hey, listen to what happened to *me* yesterday. This will make you laugh. . . ."

In frustration, the woman cries, "You just don't *get it,* Mom!"

This mother was in such a rush to soothe her daughter's pain she instantly tried to distract her and never even acknowledged her upset. That's like the fast-food order-taker jumping right to "That's five dollars, drive up front" before repeating your order so that you can confirm it.

Of course, we never want our loved ones to be sad. But failing to acknowledge their feelings only makes them feel unheard, alone, and even *more* upset!

What if the mother had handled it differently? What if she had first patiently listened to and repeated her daughter's feelings before she offered a distraction?

> *"Mom, I feel so stupid! I left some very*
> *important letters at a restaurant! My boss is*
> *going to kill me!"*
> *"Oh, no!"*
> *"My boss is so rude, I know he'll scream at me*
> *again."*
> *"No wonder you're so upset."*
> *"Yes, I'd been working on that report for two*
> *weeks!"*
> *"Nooo! All that effort!"*

*"Thanks, Mom, for giving me a shoulder to
cry on. I'll get through this somehow."*

*"You know I'm always here for you. Hey, listen
to what happened yesterday, this will make you
laugh. . . ."*

When we're upset the first thing we want from our friends is for them to hear us—lovingly and attentively. Like a waitress repeating our order ("So that's a burger and fries?"), a friend's close attention makes us feel understood and respected. Then we are usually much more open to offers of advice, reassurance, or distraction.

Door Openers: A Quick Way to Show You Care

A quick way to show an upset person that you care is by using a *door opener.*

Door openers are little gestures or comments you make in response to a person telling you his problems. They encourage the person to share his true feelings with you.

Here are a few of the little things you can do and say to encourage your friend to open his heart:

- Raise your eyebrows in surprise.
- Nod your head repeatedly as he talks.
- Say any of the following as you listen:
  "Uh-huh."
  "Sure."
  "Wow!"
  "I see."
  "Oh, no."
  "You're kidding!"
  "Then what happened?"
  "Tell me more. . . ."

The next time you're watching TV, pick out one of the characters and watch her really carefully. Notice the normal turn-taking that goes on in the dialogue. Now notice, when the character gets upset, how the other characters respond to her. Do they: ignore? criticize? distract? immediately reassure? Or do they first respectfully acknowledge her feelings (the FFR)?

Notice, too, that good listeners never ask a person who is crying and obviously upset, "Are you sad?" They just caringly describe what they observe: "I can see how upset you are!"

Okay, now on another day, watch some kids in a park. Notice when they get upset how their parents respond. Do they: ignore? criticize? distract? immediately reassure? Or do they first respectfully acknowledge the feelings (the FFR)?

This exercise will really make you more aware of the power of the right (or wrong) reaction. Pretty soon you will become your friend's favorite person to talk to!

FFR Part 2: What You Say Is Not as Important as *the Way You Say It*—Finding the "Sweet Spot"

Most people think that *what* we say is the key to good communication. Of course, words are very important, but when you're talking to someone who is upset (mad, sad, scared, etc.), *what you say* is much less important than *the way you say it*.

Big emotions trip up our brains! They make our logical left brain (the side that understands *words*) stumble and stall while allowing our impulsive right brain (the side that focuses on *gestures* and *tone of voice*) to hijack the controls.

So when we're upset, we need someone to respond in a way that will get through to our right brain. That's why if you pour your heart out to a friend and she just parrots back your words with a blank face and a flat voice, you'll end up feeling even worse. Even if your listener's words are totally accurate, if they're spoken in an emotionless way, you'll end up feeling like she just doesn't "get it," and that will make you feel even worse.

Now that you know how to echo an upset person's words (FFR Part 1), you're ready to learn how to put some emotion into your words so your friend feels understood and cared about. Mirroring the right amount of emotion is super-important. Use too little and your friend will feel you don't really get it. Use too much and she'll think you're being hysterical or making fun of her. I call mirroring just the right amount of emotion "hitting the sweet spot."

To hit your upset friend's sweet spot you should try to reflect about one-third of her emotional intensity in your tone of voice, face, and gestures. Then, as she calms, you can gradually return to a more normal way of talking.

Hitting the Sweet Spot

Here's an example to help illustrate the importance of hitting the sweet spot.

Imagine you just got fired and you go to see a friend so that you can pour your heart out. Which of these scenarios would make you feel the most cared about and comforted?

- Your friend, who happens to be a robot, sits perfectly still and mechanically acknowledges your troubles: "Carol . . . that-is-ter-ri-ble. . . . You-must-feel-so-sad."
- Your friend, a drama queen, wildly waves her arms, eyes bugging out in horror, as she blurts, "Oh, no! That's horrible! You'll starve!"

Probably neither! The robot's emotionless delivery feels cold. The hysteric reacts with such a flood of emotion that she may make you feel even more lonely and misunderstood. Most of us prefer our friends to respond with words and gestures somewhere in the middle range of intensity.

- Looking concerned, your friend sighs and says sincerely, "Oh, noooo. Oh, Carol . . . Oh, noooo." That may not be terribly eloquent, but it's deeply comforting because your friend's tone and expression let you know that she is sympathetic and respectful of your pain. She has connected with your sweet spot.

With a little practice, you'll find that hitting the sweet spot will become as easy and automatic as returning a smile.

Tips for Finding the Sweet Spot with People of All Ages

In general, a person's sweet spot is a couple of notches *lower* than her level of agitation. But it varies from one person to the next. For example:

- Toddlers have really big emotions, so they usually need us to be more demonstrative to reach their sweet spot.
- Shy kids and adult men tend to be less emotionally expressive and may even feel mocked if their feelings are mirrored too closely. They do better when we underplay our response and aim lower to find their sweet spot.
- Teens can be very dramatic, but they don't like *us* to be dramatic when we acknowledge their feelings. So "aiming low"—by being caring, but a bit subdued— is usually the best way to hit their sweet spot.

Sylvia told Carla that she could see she was really, really mad, but she did it in a silly, singsong voice that made her three-year-old even madder! When she thought about it, Sylvia realized that by trying to distract Carla and make her laugh at herself for getting so upset, she had prevented Carla from feeling heard and respected. Amazingly, when Sylvia said the same words again, but in a tone that reflected just a bit of her daughter's upset, Carla quieted in seconds and looked up at her mother with real appreciation.

Practicing the FFR

The easiest way to master this new style of responding is to try it out with a friend who is just *a little* upset. Narrate your friend's feelings with a bit of caring emotion on your face and in your voice. Then, as you get more comfortable with the technique, try using it with someone who is very upset.

New habits take time to learn. So don't worry if you find you keep forgetting to use the FFR at first. Before you know it, you'll be amazed by how many compliments you get for being a great listener, a great friend, and a great parent.

Common Questions About Using the FFR with Children

Q: Don't I get to speak first? After all, I am the parent.
A: Of course your child must respect you, and you'll have many opportunities to teach her that. But when she's upset, insisting that she wait for you to talk first will make her feel unloved.

We're forever reminding kids to wait their turn. Well, the best way to teach that is to practice what we preach.

Q: I find the Fast-Food Rule a bit unnatural. Will I ever get used to it?
A: Like any new skill, it takes practice. But most parents find that the FFR becomes almost automatic after just a week or two.

Q: If my child falls and doesn't cry, do I have to use the FFR?
A: The FFR says to mirror a bit of your child's response. So if your child doesn't seem upset about the fall, just casually comment, "Wow! You fell. That was a big boom."

Q: Should I use the FFR when I think my son's complaints are unreasonable?
A: Initially, yes. You'll have an easier time getting him to respect *your* view if you first let him know that you see *his* side of things.

Q: Do I ever get to give my message first?
A: Sure. Remember, the FFR says, "Whoever is most upset goes first." Usually that's your toddler, but *you* go first if she's in danger, being aggressive, or breaking an important family rule (see Chapter 7). After all, in those situations you're the one who is most upset.

So if your daughter runs into the street when she's having a tantrum, *you go first*! Run and grab her and say, "*No! No street! Danger!*" Then, once you're safely back on the sidewalk, you should take a minute to acknowledge her feelings.

Emotions and learning are like oil and water . . . they don't mix! That's why the moment when your toddler is struggling to escape the car seat is *not* the best time to give him a lecture about deaths on the highway. Even adults become more unreasonable and illogical when we're upset. So it should be no surprise that your toddler can't hear you until the tidal wave of his emotions starts to subside. When your child enters *caveman mode,* energetically acknowledge his dismay, and then, once he calms a bit, you can try to distract him, reassure him, or solve the problem. Here are some other things you might do and say when it becomes *your* turn:

- **Be physical.** Offer a hug, tousle his hair, put a hand on his shoulder, or just sit quietly together.
- **Whisper.** Whispering is a fun way to change the subject and reconnect.
- **Give options.** "We can't have soda, but how about some yummy juice?"
- **Explain your point of view . . . briefly.** Save important lessons for a calm time, later on, when he can pay better attention.
- **Teach how to express feelings.** "Make a face to show me see how sad you are," or "When I'm mad, I stomp my feet, like this. . . ."
- **Talk about how emotions feel, physically.** "You were so mad, I bet you felt like your blood was boiling!" or "When I'm scared, my heart goes *boom boom* like a drum."
- **Grant your child's wish . . . in fantasy.** (This is one of my favorites.) "I wish I could *vroom* up all

the rain and we could go outside and play right now!"

- **Give a "you-I" message.** Once the dust settles and it's your turn to talk, *very briefly* share your feelings using a "you-I" sentence to help your toddler learn to understand the feelings of others: "When you kick Mommy, I feel mad!" or "When you call me 'stupid,' I feel very sad inside."

The Famous Parental "But"

"I know you want to leave, but . . ." Parents commonly use the word "but" to mark the end of their upset child's turn and begin their own. If your tot resists leaving the park, try first repeating her feelings for ten seconds or so: "You say, 'No leave! No leave!' You *love* the park." Then, as she starts to calm, switch to your turn: ". . . *but*, we have to go. Let's hurry! Then we can play with Daddy at home!"

First you respect your child's feelings; *then* you use your enthusiasm to sweep her along to the next activity.

Did you know that emotions make us healthy? In fact, the way in which you react to your child's expression of emotion will contribute greatly to his health—and happiness—for the rest of his life. That's why the Fast-Food Rule is so important.

However, there's a huge and important difference between *emotions* and *actions*. While many actions are unacceptable, *most* feelings are legitimate and should be promptly acknowledged (with the FFR).

Of course, you will often have to stop your toddler's unacceptable actions (fighting, rude words, etc.). But when his strong feelings (anger, fear, frustration, etc.) are ignored or squelched, they don't just *disappear*. They continue to simmer under the surface—sometimes for an entire lifetime.

Bottled-up feelings can lead to a profound sense of loneliness ("No one understands"/"No one cares") or even bursts of hysteria (think drama queen or someone needing anger-management classes). Kids whose words of fear and frustration are repeatedly silenced may grow up *emotionally disconnected* (like the guy who snarls "I'm NOT angry!", totally unaware that the veins are popping out of his forehead).

And that's not all. Unexpressed emotion can also contribute to headaches, colitis, depression . . . perhaps even arthritis and cancer!

On the other hand, when we "have a good cry" we feel and think better. Venting anger with a good scream or punching a pillow can lower our blood pressure and help us recover, forgive, and move on. Laughter and tears have even been shown to strengthen the immune system and help heal illness.

Children whose feelings are lovingly acknowledged during the toddler years grow up emotionally intact. They know how to ask their friends for help and how to support others in need. They seek out healthy relationships, avoiding bullies and choosing confidantes and life partners who are thoughtful and kind.

Respect: As Important as Love

The magic of the Fast-Food Rule is that it conveys your sincere respect. Respect is not some modern, "airy-fairy," politically correct concept. It is *essential* to good relationships. (Of course, love is important too, but disrespect can make even loving relationships crumble.) And to *get* respect . . . you must *give* respect. That is why one of the first things all ambassadors are taught in their training is how to listen and speak with respect.

Respect does not mean letting your toddler run wild. You will often have to enforce your parental authority. But when you are both firm and respectful, you will be modeling to your child exactly the behavior you want to nurture in *her*.

Don't worry if it takes you a little time to get the hang of this new way of communicating. Even if you only do the FFR once a day . . . that's a great start. And, like riding a bicycle, the more you practice it, the more comfortable you'll get. I guarantee that soon you'll feel like you've been using the FFR your entire life.

 Use the FFR to Replace Some Old Bad Habits

Many of us would never make it as order-takers at Busy Burger. That's because too often, we *cut in line* in front of our little child to give *our* message without first acknowledging his feelings.

Perhaps we feel that our busy schedules—or our wish to make our toddlers feel better fast—justify our pushing their feelings aside and taking a turn first. We don't *mean* to be rude. But that's how it feels to a young child when we skip the FFR.

Throughout time, parents have used all sorts of techniques to stop their kids in the middle of what should be *their* turn. For example:

Threatening: "Stop whining or we're leaving."

Questioning: "What are you afraid of?"

Shame: "How dare you yell at Grandma!"

Ignoring: Turning your back and leaving.

Distracting: "Look at the pretty kitty in the window."

Reasoning: "But, honey, there are no more cookies."

Did your parents say these things when you were growing up? How did they make you feel?

Here are the four most frequent bad habits we fall into when we "elbow" our tot's feelings aside so we can take the first turn:

- criticizing with hurtful words
- making unfair comparisons
- trying rude distractions
- rushing to "make it all better"

As you develop your skill with the FFR, you'll drop these like four hot potatoes!

"Kimmie, you're as stubborn as a mule!"
"You're a scaredy-cat."
"Why are you so hyper?"
"Don't be dumb."

No parent gets up in the morning thinking of ways to crush his child's confidence with ridicule and sarcasm. That's why I'm always amazed to see parents assaulting their kids with words like "retard," "idiot," and "whiner"—words they'd *never* allow a *stranger* to call their child.

Name-calling becomes increasingly hurtful to kids around two years of age because middle toddlers are superfocused on words and they care a lot about what others think.

Often, angry words slip out on a momentary impulse . . . perhaps echoing mean names thrown at us long ago. (Can you remember being called names when you were growing up? What were they? Does thinking about them still bring up feelings of anger or hurt?)

Verbal attacks can scar like knives. Insults can brutalize a child as much as slapping him. A few cruel remarks can wipe

---

Exaggerations Kill (. . . the Spirit, That Is)

Sweeping statements like "You're the *worst!*" "You *never* help!" or "You *always* whine!" are exaggerations, and as such, they are usually unfair and *always* untrue. They make a person feel insulted and demoralized and often lead to resentment and less cooperation!

I recommend you toss the words "always," "never," "best," and "worst" right out of your vocabulary.

out a hundred hugs and trigger burning resentment or feelings of worthlessness. And what's even more outrageous is that these names . . . are always *lies*! Calling your child a "meathead" is a lie because it focuses on a momentary screwup but ignores the fifteen times he did things well.

So when you're angry, please skip the yelling and profanity and instead tell your tot how his actions made you feel: "You broke my favorite picture frame, and now Mommy is mad, mad, *mad*!"

Remember: like an ambassador, you are building a long-term relationship. Can you picture a diplomat telling a king, "You're so stupid!" or "Shut up!"? Diplomats keep a cool head and a respectful tone even when they're mad, because they know that today's enemy is tomorrow's friend.

Reframe That Name!

Fortunately, compliments and kind remarks also live long in our minds. So replace mean labels that tear your toddler down with descriptions that build him up. It's one of the best gifts you can give.

Labels that hurt	Descriptions that help
bossy	a leader
defiant	brave
hyper	energetic, spirited, passionate
nosy	curious
picky eater	discerning, knows exactly what he likes
shy	careful, looks before she leaps
slowpoke	thoughtful, deliberate
stubborn	tenacious
whiny	outspoken

Unfair Comparisons

How do you feel when someone says, "Everyone else can do it, why can't you?"

Most of us hate being compared to others, especially when it's being done as a put-down:

- "Why can't you act more like your sister?"
- "Stop it! None of the other kids are making such a big fuss."

Sand Castle of Confidence

Besides being unfair, there are two other big reasons why you should avoid using comparisons to make a point: Before you know it, you'll be trying to *stop* your child from imitating some of the *bad* things that other kids do. And goodness knows you'll hate it when she starts pointing out how her friend's parents are nicer than you!

Rude distraction

Distraction works well with babies, so it's natural to want to use it with toddlers. But be careful. To an upset toddler distraction may feel like a disrespectful interruption or like you're saying, "*Stop* feeling your feelings."

Tara, 14 months old, was thrilled with her new skill—walking. But she was *not* thrilled to be stuck in my exam room. She headed straight for the exit. "Unghh! Unghh!" she grunted, pushing at the closed door. Then she started slapping it. She wanted out!

Tara's mom, Simone, briefly acknowledged her tot's feelings, then moved directly to distraction: "No, sweetheart. I know you want to leave, but we have to stay here just a little longer. Hey, let's look at this pretty book." Unfortunately, Simone's attempt was met with a beet-red face and a shriek that rattled the windows.

Regaining her composure, Simone tried to engage Tara with a cheery verse of "The Itsy-Bitsy Spider." But again she was met with fiery protests and flailing limbs.

Frustration growing, Simone put her foot down. "Tara! No screaming! Shhhh!" But it was too late. Tara was hysterical. Embarrassed—and annoyed—Simone apologized, tossed her "little

volcano" over her shoulder, and, avoiding the
stares of the parents in my waiting room, sped
out the door.

To understand Tara's reaction, imagine that you told your best friend about something that upset you, and she responded with a silly change of subject: "Hey, look. New shoes!" I bet pretty soon you'd be looking for a new best friend.

Toddlers also get annoyed when we answer their protests and upsets with distractions. But of course, they don't have the option of switching parents. So they either accept your distraction, pushing their hurt feelings deep inside, or scream louder, to try to *force* you to care.

I used to witness this parenting faux pas in my office every day. A toddler cried as I started to examine her ears and her mom instantly started jiggling a doll inches in front of her face, chirping, "Look! Pretty dolly!"

The response? More times than not, the child's shrieks jumped an octave, as if to say, *"Dolly!? Are you kidding? Don't you see I'm scared?"*

Rushing to "Make It All Better"

We often interrupt our child's complaints with positive comments like "It's not so bad" or "You're okay."

It's natural to want to comfort your upset child. You just want to "make everything better." But when your little one is upset, immediately saying "It's okay!" can actually make things worse. That's because repeating "It's okay" over and over again may inadvertently give your child the message that you want her to stuff her feelings deep down inside and *act* happy even if she isn't. And that is absolutely *not* okay.

Monica was preparing a snack for little
Suzette—a smiley face made out of grapes,
cheese cubes, and crackers.

One day, as a surprise, Monica got even more
creative than usual. Instead of whole crackers for
the body, she broke them into strips to make
arms and legs. But when her 20-month-old saw
the broken crackers, she went ballistic.

Monica was so stunned she forgot the FFR
and rushed right into trying to make it better,
saying, "It's okay, it's okay . . . it's okay!" But
Suzette screamed even louder. With snack time
skidding into chaos, Monica found herself

repeating, "It's okay, it's okay" in an increasingly frustrated and angry voice. In response Suzette just kept shrieking, as if to say, "No, Mom! It's NOT okay! It's NOT okay!"

Please, save your reassurance for *after* you respectfully reflect your child's feelings (FFR) and she starts calming down. Saying "It's okay" only makes sense once the child really *is* starting to feel okay.

Of course, you should immediately help your little one if she's in pain or terrified. But toddlers are not delicate flowers who need to be protected from all frustration. Challenging situations strengthen a child's character and resilience. As Wendy Mogel says in her book *The Blessing of a Skinned Knee,* a child's struggles have a valuable silver lining—they boost her ability to handle life's inevitable frustrations.

Don't misunderstand me: Distraction and reassurance are great—*but only when it becomes your turn.* Farmers have to plow before they can plant, and parents need to reflect their child's feelings (and wait for them to start settling) before taking a turn.

Help Your Toddler Express Feelings

Young toddlers (12–24 months): Model for your child how to vent her feelings. For example, when she's mad stomp your feet, clap your hands, and shake your head vigorously, and teach her to say "No!" ("Evelyn says, 'No, no, no! Mine, mine! Stop now!'")

Older toddlers (2–4 years old): When things are calm, have your tot practice different faces: "Show me your happy face . . . your sad face . . . your mad face." Point out pictures in books and say "Look at that sad baby. How do you look when you're sad?" Cut out magazine pictures of people showing emotions and put them on cardboard cards or in a little "feelings book." Demonstrate *your* facial expressions so she can see what you mean: "When I get mad my eyes get small and my mouth gets tight like this [make face]."

Teach your child the words to use when she's upset. Use pictures in the "feelings book" as a starting point. Ask, "How does that boy feel? Why is that girl sad?" Enrich your child's vocabulary by using different words. For example, for "mad" you might also use: angry, furious, miffed, boiling, red-hot, etc.

Amazingly, the more you practice these simple steps, the sooner your child will start to gain control of her emotional outbursts.

Now that you are getting the hang of the Fast-Food Rule, you're ready to learn the second step in becoming the perfect "ambassador": the perfect way to make the FFR work with any toddler . . . the language called Toddler-ese.

4

"Toddler-ese":
A Talking Style That
Really Works!

"Pay attention to what you like and ignore or discourage the rest."

—Karp's law of successful parenting

Main Points:

- Toddler-ese is your toddler's "native tongue."

- You can translate anything into Toddler-ese with three simple steps: short phrases, repetition, and mirroring a bit of your child's feelings (using your tone of voice and gestures).

- The more you practice Toddler-ese, the better you get at it.

- Amazingly, all of us automatically use Toddler-ese with our young children . . . when they're happy. But we often forget to use it when they're upset.

If you were the ambassador to China but only spoke Greek, trust me, you'd have problems! Likewise, talking with your toddler will be a hundred times easier once you learn the simple steps to translate your words into his "native" language: Toddler-ese.

I discovered Toddler-ese by accident. Like most pediatricians, I dealt with twenty tantrums a day from toddlers who hated being at the doctor's. Then I began to notice that when I echoed a bit of the child's upset feelings back—using a very simple style of language—I could usually convert their crying to laughter (or at least cooperation) in minutes . . . or less!

Toddler-ese—It's Better Than Magic . . . It's Real!

Clare, a Toddler-ese fluent mom, said, "There are rare occasions when nothing settles my raging two-year-old, but my 95 percent success rate with the Fast-Food Rule and Toddler-ese is nothing short of amazing!"

Toddler-ese is better than magic—it's real and it works! It helps children feel cared about and understood. And when you combine Toddler-ese with the Fast-Food Rule, you will be able to prevent up to 90 percent of tantrums before they even happen and you'll settle more than 50 percent of the meltdowns that do occur . . . *in seconds*! (You'll be able to quickly handle the other 50 percent of tantrums by using the great skills taught in Chapter 8.)

Sound too good to be true? Fortunately, it's not. In fact, most parents who try Toddler-ese usually see major improvements in their child's behavior in just days.

A pair of two-year-olds are fighting over a ball. Shelby, the mom of one boy, kneels down, and sweetly says, "Billy, Mommy knows you want the ball and you're really mad, but it's John's turn and we have to share. Okay? Remember, we talked about sharing yesterday? You'll get a turn, I promise, but first it's John's turn. Okay?"

Would you be shocked if I told you that Shelby's wild toddler totally ignored her gentle words and lunged at the ball, scratching his friend's face and shrieking, "Mine! Mine!"

Most parents are taught to answer their toddler's screams with calm, quiet tones. It sounds kind. It sounds reasonable. Trouble is, it doesn't usually work very well.

A calm voice is great when kids are happy. But it often flops when they're upset because:

- **They can't "hear" well.** Remember, strong feelings zap the brain's language center. Crying kids see our lips moving, but our words sound jumbled to them, like gobbledygook.
- **They feel misunderstood.** Calmly refusing your tot the thing she's begging for makes her think you don't

understand how much she wants it! So what does she do next? Blasts her message—louder and harder—to get the point across! *Hmmm. Daddy doesn't "get it!" I better yell so he knows* exactly *how I feel!*

Shelby got *steamrolled* because her sentences were too long, complex, and emotionally flat. She would have been much more successful had she delivered her message in Toddler-ese.

Toddler-ese: It's as Easy as 1, 2, 3

Toddler-ese turns adult language into simple messages that our little cave-kids understand . . . even during a frenzy.

You can translate *anything* you want to say into Toddler-ese with just three simple techniques:

- short phrases
- repetition
- mirroring—a bit—of your child's feelings (with your tone of voice and gestures)

Let's look at these one by one.

Toddler-ese Step 1: Short Phrases

Toddlers are uncivilized little people. And primitive people have primitive languages. Remember those Tarzan movies? "Come, Cheetah, come!" "No, Jane, no eat."

Even adults get primitive when we're upset. That's why we say that someone who got really mad "went ape!" Strong feelings, like fear and anger, make us drop down an emotional elevator. And the more upset we get, the more primitive we become: *Ding! Going down!*

Well, the same thing happens to toddlers. Except the left half of the brain in young children starts out immature and primitive, so when they get upset, their behavior often gets absolutely *prehistoric*!

That's why the first principle of Toddler-ese is to use very short phrases. The more upset your toddler is, the more simple your words need to be.

For young tots, or very angry older kids, start with one- to two-word phrases (using just the key words). For example, for an upset two-year-old:

Instead of:	Say:
"I know you feel mad about it."	"You're mad! Mad! *Mad!*"
"Did that doggie scare you?"	"Scared! Scared! Big doggie!"
"You really want that candy, don't you?"	"Candy! Candy! You want it . . . *now*!"

These "bite-size" bits of lingo are perfect for a child's stressed-out brain. (Of course, as your tot recovers, you will stretch your phrases back to normal.)

Toddler-ese Step 2: Repetition

Repetition is just as important as short phrases. That's because upset toddlers often miss our initial words. You know the saying that adults go *blind* with rage? Well, toddlers go . . . *deaf* with rage.

Words whiz by your toddler's brain too fast for her to handle when she's in an emotional tangle. And the more upset she gets, the deafer she'll seem. That's why you'll need to repeat the same short phrase three to eight times . . . just to get your upset toddler's attention. Then, it helps to say it a few more times, to convince her you really understand.

Does this sound excessive? It's not. In fact, *many* parents fail to soothe their child merely because they think acknowledging their child's feelings just one time is enough. But when emotions slam shut the door of your child's mind, you have to "knock" many times just for her to hear you and "let you in."

Here's how to do it: Imagine it's raining, and your two-year-old, Sam, is desperate to go splashing in the mud. He's crying at the door, struggling to reach the knob. In response you:

- Get down on his level and point to the door.
- Say: "You *want* . . . you *want* . . . you want *outside*! Outside *now*! Sammy says, 'Go . . . go . . . *go!* ' "

If he keeps fussing, repeat your words a few more times. Soon he'll turn to you, as if to say, *Huh? You talkin' to* me?

As his crying lessens, stretch your sentences back to normal: "Sammy says, 'Outside now!' You really want to go out! You say, 'Let's go play, Mommy!' "

If you have voiced his feelings accurately, he'll turn to you, look you right in the eyes, and think to himself: *Bingo! That's exactly what I want. Mom "gets it"!*

As he calms a bit more, it becomes *your* turn to give a message (explanation, distraction, etc.; see page 53):

"But no, sweetheart, noooo. It's raining! *Raining! Wet . . . yucky!* Come with me! Let's have a pillow fight. *Come on!* It's fun!"

Toddler-ese Step 3: Mirror *a Bit* of Your Tot's Intensity in Your Tone and Gestures

The first two parts of Toddler-ese are a big help, but the third is the *magic key*!

Your little one may not understand all your words, but she's *brilliant* at reading your voice and face (a right-brain specialty). That's why mirroring *a bit* of your child's emotion with your tone of voice, facial expression, and body language lets you connect perfectly with her sweet spot!

- **Voice.** Use more *oomph* than normal, but speak at a lower volume than your child is using. Reflect some of the fear, frustration, and other emotions you hear in her tone of voice, at about a third of her intensity. (If your child is very shy or sensitive, you will probably have to use a bit less intensity.) Gradually bring your voice back to normal as she begins to calm.
- **Face.** Be expressive. Raise your eyebrows, shake your head, open your eyes, furrow your brow, purse your lips.
- **Body language.** Use lots of gestures. Wag a finger, wave your hands, point, shrug, stomp the ground.

A Gesture Is Worth a Thousand Words

Toddlers are really attentive to hand gestures, probably because they can gesture well before they can speak. In fact, their first communication (besides crying, giggling, and facial expressions) usually consists of pointing at something to indicate "I want it!" or "What's that?" Most 9-month-olds *wave* bye-bye, but it often takes another year for them to *say* "Bye-bye!"

In English, the pointer finger is called the *index* finger. The word "index" comes from the Latin verb *dicere,* meaning "to say." This ancient use of the hands to communicate is also reflected in Serbia, where the pointer is referred to as the *kazhi perst,* which translates as "talking finger."

Don't Go Overboard

Some parents mirror *120 percent* of their toddler's tantrum, really hamming it up. Exaggerated displays may stop a child's crying, but they work through distraction and mockery. That is *not* what I recommend. The goal of Toddler-ese is to calm children through understanding and respect. That happens by mirroring just a bit of their feelings.

Level the Playing Field

Kneel just *below* your toddler's eye level. This simple gesture shows her you respect her and you care. If you want, you can ask your child to look you in the eyes ("Give me your eyes!"), but don't try to push the issue. Children who are angry or ashamed often avoid meeting our eyes. Remember, the goal isn't to break your child's spirit. So don't force the eye contact. If you treat your toddler with respect she'll be able to look you in the eyes and return the respect to you by the time she's school-age.

Tailor Your Response to Your Child

Your child's temperament matters! Spirited kids are more emotional, so they need us to mirror more of their feeling—up to 50 percent. Shy kids are self-conscious and need us to mirror a bit less. In fact, they may feel mocked if we mirror their feelings too strongly. Age matters too. Generally, older toddlers need to be mirrored less dramatically than younger toddlers.

Fran tried Toddler-ese with her irate three-year-old, but she did it in a silly, singsong voice that made Camille even madder. When she thought about it, Fran realized that she was trying to make Camille laugh rather than make her feel heard and respected. Amazingly, as soon as Fran changed her tone to reflect the genuine distress Camille was feeling, Camille quieted in seconds!

Be a Spokesperson

When toddlers are upset, their left brains get unbalanced and they have trouble finding words for what they want to communicate. One way to help your child overcome this *speaker's* block is for you to talk *for* her. Say what you think she'd say if she could. For example:

> *If your child resists having his teeth brushed, you might say: "Siena says, 'Me do it! Me do it!' "*
> *If your child cries when the juice spills, you might say: "Brenda says, 'My juice! My juice! I want my juice!' "*

Be a Sportscaster

Another way to help your tot calm down is to describe what she is doing, as if you are a TV sportscaster "calling the action." For example:

> *If your child is having a fit, you might say: "You're sooo mad!! You're on the ground . . .*

kicking! And your face is really sad! You wanted
that toy and now you're mad at Mommy!"

Good listening is your secret weapon. Successful parents, like successful ambassadors, build great relationships by communicating with love and respect (not power and put-downs).

Think of the FFR + Toddler-ese as the "Rescue Team" that helps you save your child when she's lost in the *jungle* of her emotions. Instead of trying to *coax* her into calm with quiet tones, use some spirited Toddler-ese to connect with her. *Then,* as she begins to settle, gradually use a more normal voice to guide her back to "civilization."

Now that you know the fine points of Toddler-ese, let's go back to Shelby and the struggling two-year-olds (on page

69), and let's imagine what might have happened had she used Toddler-ese:

> Kneeling down to her son's level, Shelby put on a
> serious face, pointed at the ball three times in
> quick repetition, and using a strong voice said,
> "Ball! Ball! Ball! You want it! You want it *now*!"
> Her son calmed a bit and turned to look at her
> and Shelby continued in an energetic but caring
> voice, "But, noooo. No ball, honey. It's John's
> turn. John's turn." Billy was still frowning, but his
> shrieks had mellowed into whining. At that
> point, Shelby distracted them both: "Look! Wow!
> A jungle gym you can climb on! Wow! Come on,
> guys, let's play with that."

Of course, not all struggles end so easily, but more than half do . . . and that will make you feel pretty darn smart. (See "Stop Tantrums" on page 216!)

Toddler-ese in Action

Sounds good in theory but what about in practice? I've seen the FFR + Toddler-ese help countless parents smooth their toddler's ruffled feathers. Here are a few of their stories:

> **When Paris, a 20-month-old, whined for a cookie, here's how his dad handled it:**
> Paris: I want! I want! I waaaaant!!!!!
> Joe (kneeling down, with a serious but caring
> look, points two to three times to the jar and

says with in animated voice): You want! You want! You want! You want cookie now!

Paris (reaches toward the cookies, grunting with impatience): Unh! Unh!

Joe (points to the jar two to three times in rapid succession and echoes the grunt): Unh . . . unh! You want! You want! (Paris looks right at his dad.)

Joe (in a calmer voice): Cookie . . . cookie! I know, Paris . . . but, no . . . no! No cookie now. (Opens eyes wide and, in a happy voice, changes the subject.) But, hey! Let's play ball! Come on! Here it is . . . catch it!

Here's how Iris helped her 2½-year-old reduce his tantrums:

"When Jason starts to scream, I jump in and describe why I think he's upset. If I imitate a little of his feeling in my voice and face he sees I 'get it' and he usually settles . . . quickly.

"However, if I stop the Toddler-ese too soon, his wailing starts again, and I have to go back and do a little more. 'Jason is still mad, mad, mad! He's angrrrrry! Jason says, No, no . . . no!' Your face is really mad!" When he starts to quiet and look at me, that's the signal for me to take a turn to talk and offer my point of view or some solutions.

"Initially, his tantrums would last for five to ten minutes. Now, they end in seconds! He still needs a minute to two of my attention when he's upset, but he gets back into a good mood much faster!"

For Leslie, Toddler-ese was her magic charm for survising the "diaper-wars":

> "Last night at a restaurant, Nathan, 15 months, pooped, and I had to take his flailing little body out to the car to get a fresh diaper on him. As he screamed in protest, I tried to lovingly acknowledge his feelings: 'I know you don't want to leave the restaurant. I know you don't like it.' But he was so mad and squirmy that I couldn't even change him.
>
> "In desperation, I gave Toddler-ese a try. I made fists and started to sort of beat the air, mirroring a bit of his frustration in a strong voice (but not too loud), 'You say, "No! No! No! No change, Mommy!" You hate it! You hate your pants down. It's COLD!!! You're maaaad!'
>
> "Then the coolest thing happened. He suddenly looked at me, half amused and half mischievous, and began playing with the mobile hanging from the ceiling light. (I had earlier tried to get him to look at it . . . without success.) As I changed him, I distracted him with a continuous dramatic narration about everything I was doing. He stayed happy the whole time! Then I sang a little song and I danced him back to the restaurant . . . feeling like a perfect parent!"

Worried that this sounds like a lot of work? Relax! Toddler-ese is actually a lot *less* work. Once you get the hang of it you'll be able to shorten or eliminate so many struggles that you'll save time . . . energy . . . wrinkles . . . and gray hairs.

Toddler-ese May Seem Hard . . . but You're Already an Expert!

I know Toddler-ese can feel odd at first. But would you believe that you already use Toddler-ese *all the time*? Almost all parents automatically use "Toddler-ese" when their child is . . . happy!

Imagine you're in the park and your three-year-old bravely climbs to the top of the slide . . . for the very first time. Beaming a huge grin, she shouts, "Look, Mommy! *Look!*"

Which of these two responses would feel more natural for you to make to her?

To flatly say, "Very good, mother is proud."
To applaud and chirp in your best cheerleader voice, "Yea! You *did* it! *Good* climbing! *Wow!*"

For most parents the first is too stiff, but the second feels pretty normal. Well, that's Toddler-ese! Amazingly, we instinctively automatically speak Toddler-ese when our kid does something to make us proud and happy! Too often, however, when she gets scared, mad, or sad, we suddenly become serious and stiff. Our voices get flat and ultracalm and we sound like emotional zombies, because we think that acting calm will calm our child. But this often backfires, because if we display no emotion when our child is really upset, she may feel misunderstood and alone just when she needs a friend.

It can take a little time and practice to get the hang of Toddler-ese. So, if you're just learning and still feel self-conscious talking like that, no worries—just start out slowly. Use it first for the little ups and downs. Once you get more comfortable with it, gradually start using it for more turbulent upsets. I guarantee that you will love using it.

Here's a fun way to help you see how other parents handle their toddlers' struggles. Go to a park and look for kids who are upset (if it is a busy park, you should easily be able to find several). When a child cries, listen to what the mom (or dad) says. Does she repeat back her child's upset (like the order-taker saying "Burger and fries?") or does she jump too fast to her turn, using distraction, explanation, or name-calling?

 ### "But Dr. Karp, I Sound Demented!"

Ernst and his Danish wife, Katrina, are the parents of two-year-old Rolf. A few months after explaining Toddler-ese to them, I asked if they'd tried it. Katrina said, "Toddler-ese feels funny for us—a little too dramatic. The Danes don't like to go 'over the top' like that."

Don't be surprised if you too feel a bit awkward—okay, downright *weird*—when you start using Toddler-ese . . . wherever you're from. But I hope you'll open your mind and try it anyway. I promise that your child will quickly become more patient, less defiant, and much happier.

But in case you are still feeling skeptical, here are some answers to common parental concerns that may help to ease your mind:

"It Feels Like Baby Talk."

Toddler-ese isn't baby talk. It's *toddler* talk! Sure it's immature, but when our uncivilized little kids "go ape," their language-loving left brains temporarily stop working well. That's why this simple speaking style is the best way to make them feel understood and loved.

Think of it this way: When you read to your little toddler, do you start out with books like *War and Peace* or even *Charlotte's Web*? I doubt it. The books that most tiny tykes love usually have a literary style that's no more complex than "Mmm, yummy apple" or "See Spot run!"

And besides, you'll only be using Toddler-ese during times of upset. The rest of the day you'll be chatting away with your little one in your normal style of speech. So don't worry about stunting your child's language skills; you won't.

"I Worry I'll Turn My Child into a Drama Queen."

I know that some experts warn parents that paying attention to a child who's acting up will only reinforce the misbehavior. They say we should turn away from the crying and turn back only when she stops, rewarding her self-calming with some loving attention.

I agree that kids who engage in prolonged periods of whining often need to be briefly ignored to avoid accidentally rewarding their behavior (see the Law of the Soggy Potato Chip on page 190 and **kind ignoring** on page 180). But even if your child is overdoing it and "yanking your chain," the best response is to start out by using the Fast-Food Rule—aimed at the sweet spot—to sympathetically acknowledge her feelings, and only resort to ignoring if the FFR doesn't calm her down.

The world is tough and often disrespectful or uninterested in a child's feelings. If you ignore your little one each time she's very upset, she may come to believe that you're not interested in her true feelings and learn to keep them buried deep inside.

"It Feels Like Teasing."

In the past, you may have heard people mirroring someone's feelings to mock or ridicule them. But Toddler-ese is actually the opposite of teasing. That's because the mirroring is never overdone (remember the sweet spot) and is understated and performed with genuine compassion, sincerity, and respect.

"It Feels Like I Am Giving In to Bad Behavior."

Absolutely not! Respectful listening doesn't mean caving in or being a wimp. You can be both understanding *and* a tough disciplinarian: "Shari, I know Richard took your block and you're mad, *mad, mad*! But, *no* scratch! *No scratch!* Stop now!"

Remember, there's a huge difference between angry *feelings* and angry *actions*. Yes, you have to discourage misbehavior, but it's superimportant that your child know that you understand how she feels, and you care, even if you disagree. Toddlers whose parents always acknowledge their fears and frustrations grow up emotionally healthy, feeling comfortable in their own skin.

"It Feels Embarrassing!"

Okay, I admit Toddler-ese *is* embarrassing! However, when your primitive little friend has a hissy fit in aisle six at the grocery store you're going to be embarrassed no matter what. So, really, you have only two choices:

You can be embarrassed *big-time* as you drag your child out of the store (as she's screaming and hitting and knocking things off the shelves), leaving your shopping undone and both of you mad.

Or, you can be embarrassed on a lesser scale as you get down on her level and mirror some of her upset for a minute. But with this second option, the tantrum will probably end fast, you'll avoid lingering resentment, and you can get on with your plans.

Toddler-ese may draw stares from surprised passersby, but it *works*. And when other parents see how quickly your child calms, they'll be asking you for pointers!

"It Feels Unnatural, Like I'm an Actor."

Some parents say Toddler-ese feels unnatural, artificial, overly dramatic.

But in truth, we *rarely* talk to toddlers in a normal adult style. For example, do you matter-of-factly ask your tot, "How was breakfast?" Or do you sweetly chirp, "Mmm! Yummy, huh?"

When our kids are happy and excited we naturally reflect that in our voice and expressions. And when they're a little bit sad we instinctively mirror that back in perfect Toddler-ese. So in most situations this approach feels totally comfortable. But when our kids are very upset, suddenly we forget our Toddler-ese and start speaking to them in an overly flat tone of voice because we think it will calm them down. But as far as they're concerned, *that* is what's really unnatural. And it's not usually calming or reassuring anyway.

What Do You Do If Toddler-ese Doesn't Work?

Toddler-ese is highly effective, but no single technique works 100 percent of the time. So, if you have tried the FFR + Toddler-ese and your child is still in orbit:

- First, make sure you did it right: If you missed your toddler's sweet spot (too many words, too much or too little feeling, etc.) your toddler may keep on yelling. Try repeating her feelings again (three to eight times, depending on her age and level of upset) in your best Toddler-ese to see if that will make her whining abate.
- Next, consider another strategy: If she's crying, but not being disruptive, try offering a hug, a quick solution to the upset, or kind ignoring (see page 180). However, if she's so mad that she's breaking the rules, she may need a **consequence** (like a **time-out,** see page 190).

The FFR + Toddler-ese: The Perfect Consolation Gift!

Interestingly, this approach often calms toddlers *even when we don't give them what they're screaming for.* That's because the caring and respect we show by speaking with the FFR + Toddler-ese is a gigantic consolation prize.

Here's what I mean: We must all learn that there will be thousands of things we want in life that we'll never get. That's disappointing, but we all eventually learn to deal with it. However, a much greater disappointment is to be deprived of the kindness, sympathy, and respect of the people we love.

Mastering Toddler-ese

Practice Toddler-ese When Your Child Is in a Good Mood

When your tot asks you for something (that you're happy to give), repeat his request using your best Toddler-ese. For example:

> *Your one-year-old opens her mouth and points up to your juice. You simply narrate his request in simple words, "Juice! Juice! You want juice. Okay, sweetheart, juice . . . here it is."*

Imagine How You Would Use Toddler-ese in an Upsetting Situation

Some parents find it helpful to practice Toddler-ese in front of a mirror or in their mind. For example:

> *Imagine your toddler is in the sandbox howling because his friend pushed him down. What would you say? (Remember the spokesperson and sportscaster techniques on page 76.) What kind of voice would you use? How would you use your hands and face? Once he calms down, what might you say?*

Rehearse with a Toy

After your child recovers from an upset, let him "overhear" you telling his teddy bear what just happened . . . in Toddler-ese. For example:

> *"Psst, hey, Teddy! Juan was sad! Sad! Juan's ice cream fell. Gone-gone! Ice cream gone! Then I hugged him . . . like this (demonstrate hug). Now Juan is happy!"*

Please be patient. All new skills feel odd at first. But the more you practice, the better you'll get. Stick with it for a few days and soon your little one will look at you with delight, as if to say, *"Yea! You understand! You're awesome!"*

When Does a Child Outgrow Toddler-ese?

Actually, Toddler-ese is *not* just for toddlers. It also works with older kids (and even adults), because when anyone gets really upset their eloquent left brain *shuts down* and their impulsive, impatient right brain *takes over*.

Here's how you might echo the feelings of a frustrated six-year-old: *"You say, 'Go!' You're finished with being here. Finished. You want to leave right now! And you're not kidding."* This would definitely get her attention and help defuse the situation. Then, once she calms, you would return to the more mature language you usually use.

Older kids and teens (and adult men!) are particularly self-conscious about their feelings, so you only need to mirror a little bit of their emotion to hit their sweet spot.

Patty's Story: A Parental Triumph

"The idea that our 26-month-old was a bit of a 'cave-girl' made perfect sense to my husband and me. So I tried Toddler-ese:

"One day, when Kira's shower was over, she went ballistic! I love showers, so I could sympathize. With wide-open eyes and lots of nodding I pointed to the showerhead and said, 'You want! You *want*! You *want*!! You want shower . . . *now*!' She continued yelling, so I continued a tiny bit stronger. 'You want shower! *You want shower! You want it! You want it, now!*' Almost like magic, Kira responded immediately.

"Her crying stopped and she looked at my face with a hopeful glance. Then I softly said, 'You want to *stay*! But no, nooooo. I'm so sorry, sweetheart, we need to go to school! And your dolly wants some yummy breakfast. So come on! Come on! Let's get some food! Do you want eggies or crunchies [cereal] today?'

"After one more fake cry, Kira let me dry and dress her while I discussed our exciting plans for the day.

"Now whenever Kira resists getting dressed and shouts, 'Me do!' I turn on the Toddler-ese: 'Kira says, "Me do! Me do!" You want to do it yourself!' Kira totally gets it. She nods her head and smiles with relief. And as she struggles to put on her shirt, she just lets me slide on her pants and socks.

"A bonus gift that we've gotten from Toddler-ese is that we have more fun together. It has made me feel like a genius!"

Now that you know these effective communication basics, it's time for a few more skills! The next part of the book will teach you how to increase your child's good (green-light) behaviors and how to stop the bad (yellow- and red-light) ones . . . fast!

PART THREE

Behavior Basics:

Raise a Great Child the *Green-Yellow-Red-Light* Way

Over these next three years you'll constantly be molding your child's behavior, encouraging the good and discouraging the bad. I find it helps to think of your job as being a bit like a traffic light: Flash a *green light* (Go!) to behaviors you want to continue; flash a *yellow light* (Warning!) to behaviors that are annoying; and flash a *red light* (Stop now!) to actions that are seriously unacceptable and/or dangerous. Some parents I know refer to green-yellow-red behaviors as the Good, the Bad . . . and the Ugly!

♦ **Chapter 5** will cover green-light behaviors and give you specific tips for boosting your toddler's good actions and manners.

♦ **Chapter 6** presents fast, effective, and loving ways to curb your toddler's annoying yellow-light behaviors.

♦ **Chapter 7** teaches you "take-charge" consequences that are perfect for quickly putting the brakes on your child's aggressive, dangerous, or disrespectful red-light behaviors.

5

Green-Light
Behaviors:
How to Encourage
Good Behavior

"A child is fed with milk and praise."
—Charles and Mary Lamb, *Poetry for Children*, 1809

Main Points:

The best way to help your toddler behave better is to flash a
green light of encouragement every time you see him being
good. Here are five enjoyable ways to do this:

- **Time-*ins*:** Boost cooperation with bits of fun
  (includes **attention, praise, gossip, rewards,
  hand checks, star charts, play**).

- **Build confidence:** Respect—plus some silliness—
  makes kids feel like winners (includes **giving
  options** and **playing the boob**).

- **Teach patience:** Give your child two surefire ways to build self-control (includes **patience-stretching** and **magic breathing**).

- **Create daily routines:** Simple routines help kids feel smart and secure (includes **bedtime sweet talk, special time, loveys,** and pacifiers).

- **Plant seeds of kindness:** Teach manners and character through the "side door" of your child's mind (includes **fairy tales** and **role-play**).

Parents often think that if their tot has several calm days in a row, the era of outbursts must be over. ("I know she can be cooperative. . . . She did it yesterday.") Not so fast! Although your toddler's desire to be good *does* grow as she grows, Bamm-Bamm doesn't turn into Bambi overnight. You'll be teaching your child the niceties of civilization for years to come. Part of the secret of helping your child become happier, better behaved, and more fun to be with is figuring out how to encourage her good (green-light) behaviors.

How to Raise a Toddler You Love to Be With

By the 1920s, Andrew Carnegie was one of the richest men in the world. When asked his secret of success, he said life was like a gold mine: Ignore the dirt . . . focus on the gold and keep every scrap you find. Soon, you'll have pockets full of treasure.

Success with a toddler is also like mining gold. If you worry less about the "dirt" (punishing his bad behavior) and focus more on the "gold" (all his good acts), you'll soon find you've raised a child who shares, cares, and treats people with respect.

You'll notice that this is the longest chapter in the book. That's because there are so many effective techniques for boosting desirable behavior. And the more time you spend encouraging the good, the less time you'll have to spend dealing with the bad.

Feeding the Meter Gives the Green Light to Good Behavior

You are the rock star in your child's life. And because she loves spending time with you so much, you'll find that giving her many short periods of focused attention throughout the day will soon dramatically boost her good behavior. I call this feeding the meter.

Some days it's hard to see your tot's sweetness under all the grunting and pushing. But around 15 months, your toddler will develop some great new traits that "stack the deck" in your favor:

- **Developing a more mature brain.** Between 18 and 36 months, your child's reasonable, sentence-speaking, impulse-controlling left brain will start to kick into gear. Increasingly, the blessed trait of patience will appear and his behavior will improve from *take and take* . . . to taking turns!
- **Wanting to imitate you.** You are supersmart and cool in your toddler's eyes. That's why your 18-month-old loves to watch and imitate *everything* you do, from sweeping the floor to showing kindness. (Be careful, they imitate swearing, too!)
- **Caring how others feel.** Your toddler's desire to hug an upset friend is a big growth step from self-centered baby to caring child. He now wants to do the "right thing" to please you. And his new love of pets, dollies, and friends will eventually grow into true compassion.

> *Sara was crying because of bad news she'd just gotten on the phone. When her two-year-old, Max, saw her sadness, he offered Sara his teddy bear and patted her back. Sara was amazed.*

- **Liking order (even rules).** Your tot may be a wild child, but now he's a wild child with a plan! For example, around 18 months, kids start to enjoy putting all the cars in one pile and the horses in another. Unfortunately, this love of order can also get quite rigid. At this age, some kids scream if they're given a cracker with a broken corner, and they often insist on reading the same books—in the same order—every single time.

Here's where the name comes from: "Feed" a parking meter with a coin every thirty minutes and you'll *never* get a ticket! Likewise, when you "feed" toddlers dozens of little bits of fun and attention all day long, you'll rarely have to deal with bad behavior. They just automatically behave better.

> After dinner, Mary used to spend 40 minutes cleaning the kitchen before playing with her two-year-old, Ethan. But he started to get more and more cranky waiting for his playtime. Mary solved the problem with a flash of genius! How? By "feeding his meter"! She stopped her chores after just 20 minutes, before he got upset, played with him for five, then finished the dishes and spent another 15 minutes of cuddly fun with her son before bed.

Feeding the meter flashes a big green light to a child, saying, *I like what you're doing. . . . Keep it up!* And the more you encourage cooperation, the more you get.

Green-Light Skill #1: Time-Ins

> *Boost cooperation with bits of attention, praise, and play.*

I'm sure you've heard of **time-*out*** (where a misbehaving child is made to sit alone). Well, **time-*in*** is just the opposite. It's when a well-behaving child is given tiny bits of play and encouragement. Experienced parents and teachers know that a steady stream of time-ins is a much more effective way of raising a happy, cooperative child than a steady stream of time-outs!

There are many types of time-ins. I'd like to talk to you about three of my favorites:

- attention
- praise
- play

Time-Ins: Attention

When we think of encouraging good behavior, we naturally think of praise. Praise is great, and I'll discuss it in just a minute. But even more important is just paying a little attention!

What It Is: Showing your child you're interested in what he's doing makes him feel great. (Remember, you're his rock star! How would you feel if your idol watched you do something with genuine interest?)

Best Used For: All toddlers, all day long!

How to Do It: Think in terms of bite-size bits. (You don't have to stay glued to your toddler's side 24/7.) Here are ten easy ways to feed the meter with just a look, a touch, or a few words:

- Sit with her and quietly watch . . . with interest.
- Wink.
- Smile.
- Raise your eyebrows and nod your head in pleasant surprise.
- Give a thumbs-up sign.

- Give a hug.
- Tousle her hair or touch her back.
- Shake hands or give a high five.
- While watching him, say, "Hmmm" . . . "Uh-huh" . . . "Wow."
- Briefly describe what she is doing.

Massage (A Very Special Type of Attention)

Lavish your toddler with loving touch! Touch is a rich "food" for growth. Your toddler could easily live without milk, but he'd be scarred for life without loving touch. (I agree with the noted psychologist Virginia Satir, who said we all need four hugs a day for survival, eight to stay calm, and twelve to grow stronger.)

> *"When Abigail was one month old, we began using massage to calm her fussies. Soon she became happy as soon as she heard me rubbing the massage oil into my hands!*
>
> *"We've massaged her almost every day since then. Now at 18 months, she says, 'Rub, rub!' after her bath. It's our special time. Best of all, a little massage helps even the wildest days end on a loving note."*

The skin is the body's largest body organ, and it's deliciously sensitive. So a nightly massage is a precious gift to your child. It soothes muscles, boosts immunity, prepares for sleep, and teaches gentleness and intimacy. (And, as an extra bonus, giving a massage automatically lowers *your* stress, anxiety, and depression.)

Massage is not just a mechanical act. It's an exchange of love. Cherish this time. It will become a treasured memory for you both.

Example:
> "Hmmm, you're pushing the truck! Bang! Right
> into the teddy bear." (You can even add a dash of
> praise: "You're good at playing with trucks!")
> Then go about your business for a little bit while
> he happily continues to play.

Time-Ins: Praise

Sprinkling praise throughout the day is a great way to boost green-light behaviors. But praise can backfire if it's done incorrectly. Here's how to make your praise really count:

■ **Give a "balanced diet" of praise.** Think of praise as a yummy casserole you feed to your child: lots of plain noodles (calm attention) and a big cup of tasty sauce (mild praise and encouragement) topped with a sprinkle of tangy cheese (cheers and celebration).

Kids need a balanced diet of praise, because parents who always hype it up ("You're the *best* boy in the world!") may end up with toddlers who either mistrust praise or need constant applause to feel a sense of self-worth.

■ **Praise the action you want to encourage . . . not the child.** When you help with the dishes, would you rather hear "Thanks for scrubbing the pots, that was really helpful" or "You're my best helper ever!"?

I recommend the first because, "You're my best helper" may be true one day but false the next (when your child refuses to help). On the other hand, "Scrubbing the pots really helped" is

100 percent true and it highlights *exactly* the behavior you want.

■ **Praise good *tries*.** Cheer your child on when he tries, even if he doesn't quite succeed ("Good try pouring the milk!"). You'll see steady progress, and he will feel like a success every step of the way.

■ **Don't give praise . . . then yank it back.** *"Good. You picked up your toys. Now, why did I have to nag you to do it?"* Ugh! Psychologists call this "praise spoiling," and we all hate it. It's like getting a gift, then having it yanked right back. It teaches kids to never trust a compliment.

Time-Ins: Gossip

Gossip is one of my favorite ways to green-light good behavior.

What It Is: Gossip means saying things out loud near your child, so he overhears. It works so well because all of us (kids and adults) are more likely to believe something if we *overhear* it than if it's told directly to us. Gossip makes your praise five times more effective. (And it makes your words of criticism have five times more impact too.)

For example, if a friend says, "You look beautiful," you might just brush it off as a polite remark. But if you accidentally overhear her saying this to someone else, you'll probably grin and take it to your heart. (After all, you overheard it, so it wasn't said to "butter you up.")

Not only do we tend to believe things we overhear, but when those comments are *whispered*—like a secret—we believe them even more.

Best Used For: Toddlers once they have reached the age of 15 to 18 months. That's when they begin to understand that people whisper when they're saying something extra important.

How to Do It: Let your child overhear you praise him . . . *in a loud whisper.*

> *One day Louise brought her three-year-old to me for a sore throat. Rather than battling Turner to open his mouth, I used gossip. Leaning toward Louise, I loudly whispered, "I really like it when*

Gossiping

- With your toddler nearby, whisper some praise about her to someone else. You can whisper it to anybody—even a doll, or someone you pretend to be talking to on the phone. Don't wink or look at your child when you do this. Gossiping *only* works when he thinks you don't want to be overheard.
  Cup your hand alongside your mouth and, in a loud whisper, say to the birdies outside, "Psst . . . hey, Mr. Birdie! Lauren ate *all* her peas! Yeah . . . every one!" Then turn back to your child like nothing happened and give her a little understated praise. "Good eating, Lauren!" Even if your tot doesn't understand all your words, your admiring tone of voice will make her feel valued!
- If your child leans in to listen, whisper more quietly . . . like you're telling a juicy secret. For an older toddler, mumble some of the words so he can't hear them all. This really makes it seem like you don't want to be overheard. If he gleefully exclaims, "I hear you!" just say, "Oh, it's nothing. I'm just talking to Mr. Birdie."
- Later on, repeat the *same* compliment to someone else. Your child will be pleased and think, *Wow, this* must *be true, because I'm hearing it a lot lately.*

Turner opens his mouth and shows me his big
lion teeth."

As I spoke, I cupped my hand next to my
mouth, like I was telling a secret (I kept my
fingers spread a bit to let him see my open
mouth, so he knew what I wanted him to do). A
few seconds later, when I switched on my light,
Turner immediately opened wide . . . like magic!

Time-Ins: Little Rewards

Small gifts can grease the wheels of cooperation. Some critics
disapprove of giving kids "rewards." They say, "Children
should obey simply out of respect." Nice idea, but expecting
toddlers to cooperate purely out of respect is like expecting
patience from a baby. It's not going to happen.

What It Is: Little rewards (incentives) are small gifts we give
to acknowledge when a child does something we like. Rewards
are not the same as bribery. Bribery is done to discourage *bad*
behavior . . . incentives encourage good. Of course, *you* are
your child's number one reward. His favorite gift will be a little
roughhousing, an insect hunt, playing tag, or story time. But
occasional small incentives like stickers, poker chips, hand
stamps, or a bit of candy can have a magical effect.

Wait! Did he just say "candy"?

Sweets used wisely—and infrequently—are a powerful reward for toddlers. But please don't worry. Using a lollipop or
animal crackers as an *occasional* treat won't cause obesity or
lead to a life of dessert-mania.

Best Used For: All toddlers.

How to Do It: Say changing diapers is a daily struggle. Stand your tot on the table and take out a little reward, like a special "diaper cookie" (only given during changings). Offer half the cookie when you start the change and half in the middle. Usually, within days, the struggle will diminish.

A few days later, begin to withhold the second piece until after the diaper change is complete. After another week, reduce the reward to just a half-cookie when you're done. Eventually, you won't need the cookie any longer. (Of course, you will still have to change that diaper as quickly as possible . . . after all, half a cookie will only keep a caveman still for so long!)

In addition to giving the cookie, reward his cooperation by feeding his meter with some cheery praise and a minute or two of play right after the diaper change. Your loving time-ins will be the top reward for him long after the cookie tactic is phased out and forgotten.

Time-Ins: Hand Checks

What It Is: You know how kids love hand stamps and tattoos? Well, child development whiz Dr. Barbara Howard suggests rewarding toddlers with a pen check mark on the back of the hand when they do something good.

Hand checks are great because kids notice them all day and are reminded of what a good job they did.

At bedtime, count the checks and recall what he did to earn each one. He'll end his day feeling like a winner! (Also see bedtime sweet talk, on page 129.)

This idea is easy and effective, and it doesn't cost a penny.

Best Used For: All toddlers.

What It Is: A star chart is a great way to use a little reward to feed an older toddler's meter.

Best Used For: Ages two and up.

How to Do It:

- **Pick three behaviors to focus on.** Pick two your child already does (like washing his hands or brushing his teeth) and one he's not doing (like eating some broccoli or picking up his toys). Choose goals that are very specific. For example, telling him to say thank you is much clearer than saying "Be polite." And "No fighting at school" is clearer than "Be nice to the other children."

- **Explain your plan.** During a calm moment, sit your child down and discuss some things that he's done well lately; then mention your plan for helping him do even better: "Honey, I love lots of things you do, but I want to help you do some other things." Tell him the three things you want him to do each day. Let him know that every time he does one, he'll get a star.

- **Prepare for success.** Draw a two-week calendar on a large piece of paper. Let your child help decorate it with his drawings or pictures from a magazine. Then take him shopping and let him choose his favorite stars or stickers. Involving your child in the project will get him excited about succeeding . . . and it makes it *his* star chart.

When your child meets a goal, let *him* put a star on the chart. Boost the effect of the chart by gossiping about your tot's success.

Give bonus stars for special cooperation, and ask your child what his special little reward should be for every ten stars he earns (funny stickers, poker chip, cookie, etc.).

Kids are proud of their charts. Display yours where your child (and everyone else) can see it. He'll get a dose of "visual praise" every time he walks by and *sees* his success.

Redo the chart every two weeks and add new behaviors to be rewarded as your child does better and better with the old goals.

Praise for Different Ages and Stages

Let your praise style "grow" as your child grows:

- **Early toddlers (12 to 18 months):** Be generous with praise. Use lots of smiles and a little applause and a few happy words (repeated over and over).
  Example: Cheer, "Yea! You came *so* fast . . . *so* fast! Yea! Sooooo fast!"
- **Middle toddlers (18 to 36 months):** Scale back the over-the-top praise. Occasional applause is fine, but mostly you'll smile, nod your head, and toss out bits of modest praise.
  Example: "Hmmm . . . you built a *tall* tower."
  Gossip, hand checks, and stickers are like gold and jewels to middle toddlers.
- **Older toddlers (36 to 48 months):** Older toddlers are more self-conscious. They may feel mocked or patronized if you make too big a fuss. Keep it understated and boost the effect with gossip, hand checks, poker chips, and star charts.
  A special type of praise older toddlers *love* is comparing them to something smart or powerful. For example: "Thanks for getting the keys. You did it fast as a tiger!"

What It Is: One of the biggest myths about childhood is that play is just frivolous entertainment . . . a "waste of time." Actually, play is much more important than academics during the toddler years. Play is a top toddler nutrient. When you give your child a big daily dose of "Vitamin P," you:

- thrill his senses
- help him master movement
- sharpen his thinking
- encourage his language use
- boost his people skills
- teach him about the world
- stimulate his immune system
- build his self-confidence
- improve his sleep

Do you see why play is such a brilliant way to feed your child's meter? Happy, healthy toddlers have their days filled with chasing, pretending, rolling, and tinkering.

How to Do It: There are three types of play that you should try to give your child *every day*: **outside play, creative activity,** and **reading.**

Outside Play: Kids "Go Ape" When They're Cooped Up

Some of my happiest childhood memories are of playing outside: rolling down grassy hills, kicking heaps of fallen leaves, making snowmen. (Many of us *still* revel in these activities.)

But while adults enjoy the fresh air, toddlers don't merely like it—they *need* it. A two-year-old cooped up in an apartment all day may feel as trapped as Tarzan stuffed into a tight tuxedo.

And don't be afraid to go out in "bad weather." Rain, wind, and snow add to the fun. Just get the proper clothes and shoes for yourself and your toddler and run out and have a ball!

Creative Play: Your Child's Favorite Toy—His Brain

"Imagination is more important than knowledge."
—Albert Einstein

Imagination is the key to mankind's greatest advances, from the arts to the sciences. That's why I am so sad about art classes being dropped in schools across our nation. Science and math are important, but, as the complete quote from Einstein reads, "Imagination is more important than knowledge. *For while knowledge defines what we currently know and understand, imagination points to all we might yet discover and create.*" (I know it well, because it's printed on my computer mouse pad!)

Feed your toddler's creativity with:

- **Art materials:** Go for variety: crayons, Play-Doh, collage materials, watercolors, finger paint.
- **Real—or replica—household items:** Toddlers love "monkey see, monkey do." As the months pass, they want to imitate you more and more. Use household goodies like pots/pans/wooden spoons, a toy phone, or a small broom and dustpan.
- **Props for pretend play:** Dolls and dollhouses, action figures, toy dinosaurs, and lots of costumes and dress-up clothes. By age three, a child's interest expands from imitating Mom and Dad to trying on new identities—such as princess, ballerina, firefighter, and cowboy.

- **Sensory materials:** Molding clay, a sandbox or sand table, a splash pool, a watering can, pouring toys for the bathtub, swatches of different materials (satin, velvet, corduroy, sandpaper)

Book Play: Reading Is Feeding

Want your child to have a healthy brain? Feed it . . . by reading! The key to reading with toddlers is to do it *with* them. Reading makes kids smarter, *and* it's a sweet opportunity to snuggle close and join your hearts.

- **Early toddlers (12 to 24 months):** These tots are active! So pick a reading time when your child is tired. Use books with cloth or cardboard pages. Talk *a lot* about what you see: "Look, a doggie! What does a doggie say? What do doggies eat?" Turn the book into a game: "Hey, you be the doggie. Can you bark? Wow! What other animals can we find?"
- **Middle toddlers (24 to 36 months):** Two-year-olds like things "just so." Your child may howl if you skip part of a story he's learned by heart. "Do it right!" he'll protest. As you turn each page, offer your child a chance to be smart by asking, "What's going on now?"
- **Older toddlers (36 to 48 months):** Older toddlers love stories about animals and people (and trucks!). And they love to compare what's happening in the story to situations they've experienced. "Oh, honey, Bigelow the rabbit dropped his ice cream. . . . That's like when you spilled your beans at lunch." Older toddlers repeat lines from books to their stuffed animals and even make up their own stories. Now they're at the stage when they love it if you

"accidentally" make a silly mix-up of the words. They giggle with joy when they catch *you* making a "mistake."

Is TV a Good Time-In?

Today's parents have it tough. We have lots of demands on our time, but little family support. So it's understandable when some parents flip on the TV to entertain their toddlers while they get things done.

I think of TV like candy: A little is okay every so often, but not a steady diet of it. I recommend you limit your toddler's TV-viewing time by following these guidelines:

- **Keep the TV out of your child's room.** Sadly, one in five children under age two and half of all four-year-olds have TVs in their bedrooms. This leads to too much TV watching and too many inappropriate programs.
- **Put a cap on total TV time.** Less is better! Limit your toddler's TV time to a maximum of thirty to sixty minutes a day (including videos and DVDs). And when possible, try to watch the programs with your toddler and talk about what you see.
- **Be picky.** Let your little one watch only gentle, nonviolent cartoons; toddler-oriented nature videos; and slow-paced, educational children's shows.

Green-Light Skill #2: Build Confidence

"Nothing can be done without hope and confidence."

—Helen Keller

We all know how tough it is to raise a toddler, but not many people realize how tough it is to BE a toddler. Toddlers lose *all day long*! They're weaker, slower, shorter, less verbal, and clumsier than almost everybody they know. That's why they love stomping in puddles (to make a big splash) and showing off their "massive" muscles. It's also why they can be so darn stubborn, refusing to listen or to give in.

They just want to win a few!

You can't protect your child from all the defeats he'll suffer while he's growing up. (And you wouldn't want to. They build character.) But you can help your little one become more self-confident and resilient so he bounces back from disappointments more easily.

Helping Your Toddler Feel Triumphant

This is one of the most important parenting concepts you'll ever learn: If you fill your child with many little triumphs and successes throughout the day, he'll automatically become more respectful and cooperative. Why? Because even primitive little toddlers understand the rule of fairness: *After I win a bunch . . . you get a turn.*

Think of it this way: Say you go to Las Vegas and win a million dollars. You feel great. Like a winner! Your pockets are bulging with cash. Then, on your way out, you pass a person begging. You might give him $100, maybe even $1,000. Why not? You won so much, you feel in a generous mood. It's no big deal to you. On the other hand, if you've lost your life savings, you may not even give the beggar a penny. Why? Because when you feel like you've got *nothing,* you've got *nothing* to give.

That's *exactly* how it is with your toddler. If your toddler feels like a loser all day long, he is much less likely to cooperate with you. But if you let him "win" little victories all day long, he's much more likely to let *you* win a few little struggles (such as trying a tiny piece of broccoli). He'll be thinking, *You know what, Mom? I'm such a winner today, I'm gonna let you win this one.*

Respect—and some silliness—makes kids feel like winners. That's why the best parents look for ways to help their toddlers feel smart, fast, and strong. It might be as simple (and *fun*) as letting him win a pillow fight or allowing him to choose which plate he wants to eat from.

Here are two fun ways to build your tot's confidence: Show that you believe in him, and (my all-time favorite) playing the boob.

Building Confidence: Show Your Tot You Believe in Him

The more your child knows you believe in him, the more he'll believe in himself. Here are some easy ways to boost your toddler's self-confidence. . . fast!

Listen with Respect. When you listen to your child with patience and respect, you send him the message that you really value him as a person.

Ask for Help: "Can You Carry This for Daddy?" Asking your tot for help tells him, *I know you can do it.* He'll beam with pride when he shows you how capable he is. For example, say, "Honey, my hands are sooo full, can you please help Mommy and carry my purse?"

Offer Options: "Which Ones Should We Get?" There are so many decisions to make every day; let your child make a couple of them. One-year-olds aren't great decision-makers. But by two, your tot will love being asked to choose: "Which flowers should we buy, the pink or the yellow?"

Asking your child his opinion shows him that you think he's smart and you have confidence in his choices.

Two big rules about choices:

- **Don't offer too many options.** Your toddler's immature brain may get overloaded with too many choices. "Do you want milk in the red cup, yellow cup, green cup, or purple cup?" Thirty-nine flavors of ice cream? *Tilt! Tilt!*
- **Never ask your child's choice if you plan to disregard it.** For example, don't ask him which flowers to get if you've already decided to buy the pink ones no matter what.

Let Him Work It Out: "You Can Do It!" It may take your toddler five minutes to do something you can do in five seconds, but don't rush him! Put your hands in your pockets, zip your lips, take some slow, deep breaths, and encourage his efforts. ("Wow! You're really trying hard!" "Good job, you've almost got it!") If you can refrain from hovering and jumping in, your patience and body language will give your little one the message *I trust you to figure out even tough things.*

Let him work at it, even if he gets a little frustrated. Of course, offer some help if he's really getting upset.

Building Confidence: Playing the Boob

We all pretend to be klutzes sometimes when we are playing with our kids. It makes them laugh, feel clever and strong (by comparison to their inept parent), and makes them want to be more cooperative.

Sound odd? Embarrassing? Unnatural? Well, actually it's a silly idea that's supersmart and I bet you're doing it already! Do you ever:

- Pretend you're startled when your child roars like a tiger?
- Have a little race and intentionally lose?
- Have a pillow fight and let your tot topple you with each swipe?

If you answered yes to any of those, then you're already playing the boob (and, you know how much your child loves it)! Playing the boob makes kids feel like winners—and that helps them give in faster on issues that *we* care about!

> *Twenty-two-month-old Alice loves to "blow her dad over": She puffs really hard on his chest . . . and he teeters . . . then falls onto the couch while she howls with laughter.*

I play the boob again and again when I do a toddler checkup. It usually wins a child's cooperation in minutes, or less (see story on page 119).

I beg you to spend time learning this one. This goofy-sounding idea is one of the most effective tools I know for increasing toddler cooperation and diminishing tantrums.

What It Is: The basic idea is to make your child feel smart/strong/fast/etc. by making yourself seem, well, like a bit of a "boob."

Best Used For: All toddlers, dozens of times a day. Once you get the knack, playing the boob will become your toddler's all-time favorite game. (Yours, too!)

How to Do It: Here are just a few of the wacky ways to play the boob:

- **Be a baby.** Pretend you want something your toddler has. Reach out and whine like a baby saying, "Mine, mine . . . pleeease!" Let her easily defy your pitiful request. One of my favorites is to say, "Gimme five," but then pretend to be afraid. Then I let the child give me five. If she does it gently, I thank her for being so nice. But if she whacks me hard, I hop around yelping in mock pain, "Ow! Ow! Ow! You tricked me! You tricked me! You're not fair." Then I blow hard on my hand to take away the sting. Kids howl with delight and want to do it over and over.
- **Be blind.** Pretend to search for something that's right next to you. Say, "Book! Where is my book?" When your child giggles and points to it, ham it up and exclaim, "Where? Where? I don't see it." Then finally look where she's pointing and say, "Yea! You found it! You're a good finder! Thank you."

■ **Be a klutz.** Ask your child to hand you something, but "accidentally" drop it (over and over again), saying "Uh-oh! Uh-oh!"

Before I examine a worried two-year-old, I always place a toy right on the edge of the exam table so that it falls as soon as I let go. As it drops I exclaim, "Noooo! Doooon't fall!" I do this over and over, each time pretending to be ever more careful in putting it down. I "command" the toy (or plead with it), "Pleeease don't fall!" Of course, when I let go it always falls again.

Pretty soon, the child relaxes and looks quizzically at his mom, wondering *Is this the guy you* meant *to take me to, Mom? Because I can do the thing he's bumbling with.* Usually the child laughs and wants to play with me because he sees I'm such a *boob* he doesn't need to be afraid.

■ **Be confused.** Put your shoe on your hand or wear your hat upside down. Announce that you need to see if your child's hands are clean . . . but inspect her *foot* instead. Then protest, "Hey! You're *tricking* me! That's not your hand!" Now demand, "Give me your hand!" But look in her *pocket.*

■ **Be forgetful.** Ask your child: "Do you want your green pants or the blue ones?" After he says "green," immediately act like you forgot, "Huh? What? Did you say the *blue* ones?"

Point at your child's foot and fumble for the word. Say, "Give me your . . . ummm . . . your . . . uh." Frown as if you just can't remember the word "foot." Keep fumbling and pointing. In seconds, your toddler will lift up his foot and gleefully finish your sentence, "Foot, FOOT!"

■ **Be pompously incorrect.** Loudly sing the wrong lyrics to a song, "Happy *elephant* to you!" "Happy *elephant* to you!" Your child will love to correct you . . . but act like you're *sure* you're right. ("No, those are the right words!") Or like she didn't hear you correctly, "No way! I didn't say *elephant* . . . I *said* birthday." Then sing the song with the *wrong* word again and if she corrects you again, pompously proclaim, "No way! I'm the best singer . . . IN THE *WORLD*!!!"

■ **Be a pushover.** Ask your child to do something you know he won't want to do . . . and let him win. Point to the shoes on his feet and say, "Give me your shoes, pleeease! I want shoes!" When he refuses, "beg" him, "Please! Pleeease!" Then, when he refuses again (with a mile-wide grin) throw down your hands and whine, "Okay, okay . . . *you* win! You *always* win! You win me a *hundred* times!! You never do what *I* want!"

> I once made a house call to see a baby. There, I met her big sister, two-year-old Noa. Noa was drinking juice and I playfully put out my hand and asked, "May I have your sippy cup? Pleeease?" She scowled and said, "No!" Then she turned away from me and wedged herself between her dad's legs for protection.
>
> I begged like a baby, "Please? Pleeeeeease? Pretty please with sugar on top?" She protested, "No! My cup!" I saw she was looking worried, so I backed away, smiled, and chirped, "You say, 'No! Go away, Man.' Okay, Noa . . . you win, you win! That's your sippy cup! You keep it! You keep it!"

Noa beamed and puffed out her chest. She felt like a winner! And she felt that I had treated her with fairness and respect. I know that because a minute later she took my hand and introduced me to all her dollies!

- **Be ridiculous.** Say something absurd in a sincere voice, "Want some delicious . . . mud?" or "Okay, it's dinner time. . . . You have to eat your shoe!" This will make your toddler grin and feel smart because even *he* knows people don't eat mud.
- **Be weak.** Pretend a little toy is too heavy to lift. Struggle at it, then ask for help. Or wrestle, but let your child keep wriggling out of your grasp even as you boast, "I've got you now! You'll never get away!"

Is It a Bad Idea to Let Your Toddler Think You're a "Boob"?

Not at all. Your child knows you're not *really* weak or a baby. You're his ultimate hero. You'll never lose his respect just because you goof with him a little bit. In fact, he'll love you even more for it.

Think of playing the boob as an ancient form of flattery (a fundamental tool of diplomacy). It's like buttering up the king: *"Oh, Your Lordship, you are sooooo strong!"*

Green-Light Skill #3: Teach Patience

Teaching patience is another phenomenal parenting skill that's worth its weight in gold. Patient toddlers are more reasonable, less impulsive, and slower to go on the rampage when they don't get their way.

Patience is like a muscle . . . it gets stronger with exercise. It actually strengthens the left half of the brain and speeds its development! Also, as you'll see in the next chapter, teaching patience is a great tool for eliminating annoying behaviors, like whining and nagging. Practice these skills every day and you'll be astounded at the rapid improvements you'll see.

Here are two surefire ways to boost your toddler's self-control:

- patience-stretching
- magic breathing

Teaching Patience: Patience-Stretching

All kids start out impulsive. But, amazingly, you can s-t-r-e-t-c-h your toddler's patience in just days . . . if you do it right.

What It Is: Patience-stretching is a superfast way to help grabby tots learn to be patient by expecting them to wait a teensy, tiny bit . . . then a bit more . . . and then even more.

Believe it or not, most parents teach patience in exactly the *opposite* way from the method that works the best. For example, say you're busy and your two-year-old pulls at your skirt for attention. Most of us lovingly respond, "Just a second, sweetheart," and finish what we're doing. Trouble is, this often makes your child bug you even more!

Best Used For: All toddlers (even under one year of age).

How to Do It: *Very important:* To teach patience-stretching you *must* have something your child wants (food, a toy, etc.). Once you have that, follow these simple steps:

- **First, *almost* give her what she wants.** Let's say your one-year-old interrupts you, asking for juice. Stop what you're doing and repeat back, "Juice! You want juice!" Start to hand her the juice . . . BUT . . . then suddenly hold up one finger and exclaim, "Wait! Wait! Just one second!" as if you just remembered something important. Turn away and pretend to look for something.

- **Next, the "payoff."** After just a few seconds, turn back and immediately give your child the juice, praising her, saying, "Good waiting! Good waiting!" Quickly rewarding your child's patience teaches her that waiting isn't so bad and that *Mommy always keeps her word.*

Little by little, stretch the waiting time more and more (5 seconds, then 10 . . . 30 . . . 60, etc.). If you practice this every day, your child will be able to wait a minute or two (or more) within a week. Patience-stretching will build your tot's self-control . . . one baby step at a time.

Timers help older toddlers practice patience. During a calm period, show your toddler how the timer works: "See! And when Mr. Dinger says *ding!* (make it chime) then Mommy comes back fast!"

Later, when your three-year-old starts bugging you for something, say, "Sure!" and almost give it to him, but then suddenly announce, "Wait, wait! Just one second, sweetheart! I have to go see Daddy. As soon as Mr. Dinger rings I can give you the ____!" (You might suggest that your child play or look at a book until the timer dings, but don't insist on it.)

Initially, set the timer for twenty seconds. When it rings, come right back, give your child a little praise

("Hey, good waiting!") and a check on the hand, and immediately keep your promise.

Gradually increase the waiting period to a minute or two. But every once in a while surprise him by: 1) setting the timer for just ten seconds (he'll think, *Wow, that minute goes by really fast*). 2) Giving a double reward (*"Hey, you waited so well . . . here are TWO cookies!"*).

He'll think, *Wow, waiting is cool. . . . Sometimes I even get more than I expected!*

Later in the day, *gossip* to his teddy bear about his "great waiting" and at bedtime, remind him what a good job he did being patient that day.

Isn't It Teasing a Child to Almost Give Something . . . Then Take It Away?

There is a huge difference between patience-stretching and teasing. Teasing is when you taunt a child by offering the thing he wants with no intention of giving it. "You want this, but you can't have it!"

But, with patience-stretching you *will* give your child what he wants, you're just delaying it a bit. Toddlers find this totally reasonable.

Think of it from the adult point of view:

Imagine you're approved for a $1,000,000 loan and just as the banker starts to hand you the check, he gets a phone call. So he pulls back the check and says, "Sorry, I'll be right back."

Are you angry? Probably not. You don't yell, "Where's my money!" because the banker might change his mind. And besides, you have every reason to believe that you'll get the check in a minute. So what do you do? You sit patiently, hands in your lap, *and wait*. And when you get it, you feel very appreciative and offer a heartfelt "Thank you."

Dr. Harvey in Action: How I Teach Patience in Less Than Five Minutes

At checkups, I love demonstrating how easy it is to teach patience-stretching. First I warm up the child by playing the boob (for example, by repeatedly letting him "slap me five" and yelping in pretend pain).

Once he's having fun, I say, "Give me five again," and I put out my hand, but right before he whacks me, I remove the hand and hold up one finger, saying, "Wait! Wait!" Next, I turn away and make him wait for a few seconds as I pretend to look at something, Then I turn back, I praise them ("Good waiting!"), and perhaps I reinforce the praise by gossiping to his mom ("Bobby's a good waiter!"). Finally, I let the child "give me five" again and repay his patience by hopping around yelping, "Ouch! Ouch!"

Usually in just a few minutes, I can teach even a one-year-old to patiently wait for ten seconds.

Teaching Patience: Magic Breathing

What It Is: Have you ever been so upset that someone told you to "take a deep breath"? When we are stressed, frightened,

or in pain, we automatically tighten up and hold our breath. Over time, that can lead to headaches, anxiety, even high blood pressure.

Learning how to stay calm is a very important life skill. Unfortunately, many people in our culture *never* learn it (or can only calm by eating, sleeping, watching TV, or using drugs and alcohol). Yet all adults—and children—have a powerful natural stress-reducer: simple breathing!

Just a few sloooow breaths (magic breathing) can quickly bring a sense of peace. Magic breathing helps impulsive toddlers learn to *turn their motor off.* With a little practice, your little friend can learn how to use this superb self-soothing skill anytime he's frustrated, scared, hurt, or mad. It is a self-control tool your child can use forever.

Best Used For: Toddlers over two (who can already wait patiently for a minute).

How to Do It: This skill is as simple as breathing, but before you teach your bouncy little tyke, it's important for *you* to learn it.

First, *You* Practice:
- Relax your face. When the house is quiet, turn off the phone and take two to three minutes for yourself. Sit in a comfy chair, uncross your legs, put your hands in your lap, drop your shoulders, and—most important—let the tiny muscles around your mouth and eyes get very soft and relaxed.
- Take a few slow breaths. Slowly inhale through your nose (as you silently count to five) then slowly exhale through your nose (for another silent five counts). Make a little whooshy sound as the air flows in and out, and never hold your breath.

- As you breathe in, let one hand slowly rise and as you breathe out let it slowly drop.

Practice where your child can watch. He may get curious and want to imitate you.

Now, You're Ready to Teach Your Little One:
When he comes to watch you:

- Say, "Breathe with Mommy." Start by leading him through a couple of fast breaths (two counts in, two counts out), using your whooshy sound and hand motion to guide him. Don't get frustrated if he can't do it right away. It may take a dozen tries for him to get the hang of it.
- Reward *any* breathing with encouragement: "Good breathing!" "Good following my hand." Give a hand check and immediately follow it up with a little play. (Later in the day, gossip about his good breathing to your spouse, his teddy bear, or a birdie outside.)
- Gradually, lead your child through more and slower breaths (aim for at least five breaths at a sitting). Once he gets good at magic breathing, practice it in different places and at different times of the day.

Extra Tips for Magic Breathing
- **Be a role model.** Your child will learn magic breathing faster when he sees you doing it every day.
- **Time it right.** Do it before a nap or after eating, when your tot's already a bit relaxed.
- **Pick a "magic" place.** Kids love the word "magic"! Pick a "magic" spot to sit and "magic" pillow to sit on. (It will be even more special if you tape pictures of "magic" trees or butterflies on the wall of your

"magic" spot.) He'll instantly relax as soon as he sits and starts to breathe.

- **Don't be pushy.** If he resists, offer to do something fun after his magic breathing. If he still refuses, say, "No problem." Then get busy with something and ignore him for a few minutes. Try offering the breathing again later that day and the next. If your child refuses every time, wait a month or two and try again.

- **Practice often.** Kids who practice magic breathing every day quickly become little experts at self-calming.

- **Combine breathing with play.** Even wild kids will take a few breaths when they know they'll be re-warded for it. So do a couple of slow breaths, fol-lowed by something fun, followed by a final breath or two after the play stops. This is a great way for your uncivilized little friend to learn how to *self-soothe* even after hectic play.

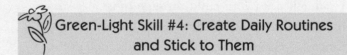

Green-Light Skill #4: Create Daily Routines and Stick to Them

Help your toddler feel safe, happy, and smart.

Doing the same thing every day may be boring to grown-ups, but for toddlers predictable routines lower stress, increase confidence, and even make them feel smarter.

Routines give little children:

- **A sense of security.** Predictable routines give tod-dlers a sense of security amid the chaos of the day. As any experienced preschool teacher will tell you, too little structure to the day makes toddlers feel over-whelmed and cranky.

- **A feeling of being smart.** Toddlers often encounter things they can't control or understand. It can make them feel frustrated and left out when they see that everyone else in the family knows what's happening. Daily routines, however, level the playing field. Tots who do the same things every day feel smart because they know what's going on . . . just as well as their older siblings and parents.

> Joan groaned when Phillip, 22 months, awoke at six A.M. and begged to watch his tractor video—every single day. But to Phillip the repetition made him feel like a genius. You could almost hear him telling himself *I knew that was gonna happen!* when he watched the tractor go through its familiar paces.

- **A sense of "time."** Predictable routines are your toddler's "wristwatch." They help her keep track of the day: *After I wake, I get dressed and eat breakfast. After lunch, I take a nap.*

Do you have little routines that raise your comfort level during the day, like a morning tea break or a call to your mom? Well, here are two fabulous routines that will make your tot feel extra-loved and extra-safe: bedtime sweet talk and special time.

Teach Your Child the Power of Positive Thinking: Bedtime Sweet Talk

Some of the sweetest moments of parenthood are our presleep snuggles with our kids. They reduce stress, build love, and

■ **Early toddlers (12 to 24 months)**: By his first birthday, your child will recognize the patterns of the day (a diaper when he wakes up, lunch when he sees you take out his special plate, a little massage before bed). Your consistency builds his sense of security, and that gives him the courage to go off and explore the world.

■ **Middle toddlers (24 to 36 months)**: Middle toddlers hate unexpected changes because they work so hard to figure things out ("C'mon! I just finally *got it*. . . . Don't go changing it on me!"). That's why routines are such a huge bonus at this age. They fill your two-year-old's need for things to "follow the rules" and be "just so."

> *Mina, two and a half, wore a princess*
> *outfit complete with wings, crown, and*
> *ballet slippers to playgroup . . . every day.*
>
> *Thirty-month-old Arnie loved his fireman*
> *hat so much that he insisted on wearing it*
> *to sleep for almost a year!*

So don't be surprised when your little kid rigidly demands the same food, same shirt, or same song every day; explodes if the peas touch the carrots or a guest sits in Daddy's chair; and insists you start over—from page one—if you're interrupted in the middle of reading her *Good Night, Moon!*

■ **Older toddlers (36 to 48 months)**: It's common for three-year-olds to suddenly notice they're weaker than almost *everybody* else. (That's why they love to point out that they are faster and stronger than babies!) Realizing that they are vulnerable can trigger new fears and worries. Routines help these kids feel safe and secure.

Despite their worries, older toddlers no longer demand rigid sameness. In fact, they love it when we throw silly variations into their routines (adding a crazy verse to a favorite song, making up new words as you read a beloved bedtime story, having a "picnic" lunch on a blanket in the living room).

provide a perfect transition from a tiring day to . . . Slumberland. You can make this period even sweeter—and more useful—with a routine called bedtime sweet talk (mentioned on page 31).

What It Is: A wonderful routine that allows you to appreciate some of the good things your toddler did today and to consider all the wonderful things that might happen tomorrow.

During the twilight moments right before sleep, your child's mind is like a little sponge soaking up your loving words. Bedtime sweet talk helps your child drift into sleep feeling smart, loved, and like a winner!

Best Used For: All toddlers. Start this loving habit as early as you can. Don't worry if your child doesn't understand all your words. . . . Even your one-year-old will be comforted by listening to your kind, soft voice.

How to Do It:
Cuddle in bed until your child is nice and relaxed, then:

- Softly retell some of his good deeds from the day (acts of kindness, fun experiences, etc.). Keep your voice gentle and understated—more like a candle than a sparkler.
- Describe the love that fills you when you watch him ("When I saw you reading, I got as happy as a puppy!").
- Count his hand checks and mention what he did to earn each one (see page 107).
- Look forward to tomorrow by mentioning a few of the wonderful things that *may* happen: "And tomorrow, at school, perhaps you'll play trains with Seymour or have fun climbing on the monkey bars. It might even be your most fun day ever! You may even

do some things that are a big help at school. . . . Teacher Kris likes it when you help pick up toys."

Here's an example of how bedtime sweet talk might sound:

> "Today was a great day. You helped water the flowers . . . and said 'Hi!' to the mailman . . . then we held hands and went to Jack's house.
>
> "And look, you got so many hand checks. One . . . two . . . three! Three checks. Do you remember what they were for? This one was for using the potty all by yourself. Oh, and this one was when you carried the mail for Mommy! And this one was for coming to the bath superfast when I called you . . . remember?
>
> "Hey, you know what I also really liked about today? When you helped Jack put away all the blocks so fast, I was so amazed, you made my heart zoom up like a big balloon!
>
> "Tomorrow could be fun too. You know, I wouldn't be surprised if Grandma shows you her watering can. . . . I bet you'll show her what a fast picker-upper you are too!"

Pack Loads of Fun into a Little Time: Special Time

Despite the many hours of time we give our kids, they often bug us the moment we start to make dinner or answer the phone. It's as if they're thinking, *Well, what have you done for me lately?*

Toddlers don't mean to be unfair. It's just that they live in the "now" and quickly forget the "before." But there's an easy, fun way to help your child remember and appreciate your time together: special time.

What It Is: Special time is a little gift of five to ten minutes of your *undivided attention.* No phone calls or baby brothers allowed! Special time feeds your child's meter with a tasty little helping of the "you-you-you" he's so hungry for.

Best Used For: Toddlers two years old and up.

How to Do It:

- **Make special time a routine.** Set aside one or two short periods every day to give your child a bit of fun. If you can, do it at the same time every day.
- **"Promote and advertise."** Kids appreciate special time even more when you stoke their anticipation and excitement. A few times a day, announce that special time is coming. "Pretty soon it's going to be special time. What fun things should we do today?" Let your tot overhear you gossiping about special time to his toys.
- **Kids get to choose.** Special time is fun because your child gets to choose the activity. If you need to, give prompts: "Ooh! Do you think we will paint or have a tea party this time?" You might read, draw, dance, hunt bugs, or have a "snowball" fight with crumpled pieces of paper. (If he wants TV, gently say, "You love TV, but TV isn't special time. Let's think of some fun things we can do together.")
- **Have a clear beginning and end.** This nugget of fun-time works best when you keep it short (about five minutes . . . set a timer). Start each session with a peppy little jingle: "It's Tony's *special* time! Special, special . . . special time!" And wind it up with a nice little ritual that you repeat every time. (For instance, say "Bye-bye, special time. See you later!" Then give a little special-time hug.)

If your child demands more time, you could give an extra minute, or you might just say, "Aww . . . I'm so sorry, honey. You love . . . love . . . *love* your special time. . . . It's really fun. But you know what? You get *another* special time later on [or tomorrow]." Then distract him and busy yourself with something else.

Think of your beginning song and ending hug as the *gift wrap* for this nugget of extra fun. It marks this time as a really special treat!

Tips for Special Time:

- **Don't do it right before naps or bedtime.** It's too fun and exciting.
- **Don't think of special time as a replacement for time you currently spend together.** It's a bite-size time-in that's offered *in addition to* the usual attention you give.
- **Don't punish your child by taking away special time.** In fact, special time can be a big help to get you and your toddler back on track if the two of you are having a rough day.
- **Don't allow interruptions.** Turn off your beeper and the phone if possible.

"Rituals" Make Routines Even More Fun

You can make routines even more fun by adding some little *rituals* to them. Rituals are small but very specific actions that add a dash of extra sparkle to your routines (like ornaments on a Christmas tree).

Here are a few rituals you might try:

- **Bedtime:** Sing a special song each night at bedtime.
- **Dinner:** Ring a bell or chime before you say grace.
- **Car ride:** Play the same song *every* time you enter the car.
- **Opening the garage:** Let your child say a "magic word" before you press the remote. ("Open sesame!")
- **Getting dressed:** Each night, put out the next day's clothes in the shape of a person.

A Daily Routine Your Kid Can Cuddle: Loveys

Linus has his blanket; Calvin has his tiger, Hobbes; Christopher Robin loves his teddy, Winnie-the-Pooh; and your child probably has his own lovey. Think of a lovey as a little "routine" your child can cuddle every day.

I've seen kids cling to diapers, silk scarves, wigs, and *all* sorts of toys. For years, my little patient Alex was "hooked" on sleeping with his Captain Hook's hook!

To some parents, cuddlies seem "babyish." But actually they are stepping-stones to maturity and independence. They help kids deal with stress (illness, trips, scary situations, etc.). And they give kids the courage to take **baby steps** from their moms and dads into the great big world. (That's why they're called "transitional objects.")

Tips on Loveys

- **Make it easy for your toddler to love a lovey.** Keep a teddy or satiny blanket near your young toddler day and night. Touch and cuddle it yourself to give it your comforting scent and invest it with *magic Mommy power.*

- **Always have a backup!** Lost loveys happen, so always have a backup that's identical to your child's *main squeeze*. (If the lovey is a blanket, cut it in two and hem it. If it's a toy, buy an extra one.) Every week or two, replace the one she's using with the spare one. That gives you a chance to keep them clean and helps them both develop the same comforting feel and smell.
- **Don't remove a lovey as punishment.** Never threaten to take away a lovey. Far from making kids behave better, it makes them resentful and insecure.

More Comforters: Pacifiers, Thumbs, Breasts, and Bottles

Sucking is another terrific, comforting "routine." It helps toddlers calm themselves—especially those who are shy or under stress. Worried parents sometimes ask me if sucking is a sign of anxiety. Not usually. Interestingly, a love of sucking is genetically passed from one generation to the next, just like hair color or freckles.

Tips on Bottles, Breasts, and Pacifiers:
- **Don't make sucking the answer to every little frustration.** You can offer a bottle, breast, or pacifier several times a day to provide some comfort, but also leave your child with daily opportunities to find other methods of self-soothing.
- **Bottles and pacifiers may cause ear infections.** That's because strong sucking can create pressure inside the ear. If your child is prone to ear infections, cut back on the bottles and pacifiers, and when she

is drinking from a bottle, be sure to keep her head up a bit. Consider switching her off the pacifier to a cuddly lovey, like a blankie, or an "auditory lovey" like a soothing-sounds white-noise CD that can be played all night long.

- **Go easy on the juice.** Fruit juice has tons of sugar. Sucking on a bottle of fruit juice for twenty minutes may cause cavities. So, if your baby loves juice, keep the sucking time short. You can also add a bit more water every day to gradually dilute it. Or better yet, switch to a naturally sweet, caffeine-free tea like mint or chamomile.

- **Wean your toddler off the pacifier by three to four years.** Sucking (especially thumb-sucking) may eventually cause buckteeth. So from time to time, mention to your tot, "When kids turn three, the pacifier fairy flies away with their old pacis and brings them back a *new toy*! I wonder what cool toy she'll bring you." (Don't say she gives pacifiers to babies. Your child might resent the next baby he sees who's sucking on what he thinks is his "old friend"!) Prolonged pacifier use doesn't always cause dental problems. Ask your doctor or dentist to check.

Green-Light Skill #5: Plant Seeds of Kindness

"Civilization is just a slow process of learning to be kind."

—Charles Lucas

Experienced parents know that toddlers often tune out our explanations and sermons (messages delivered to the "front door" of a child's mind) but pay sharp attention to what they see us do or overhear us say (messages delivered to the "side door" of the mind).

Side-door lessons allow us to sneak into our children's minds and plant seeds of kindness and good character without our little ones feeling lectured to. And practicing good behavior, over and over, through pretend play is just as powerful a teacher to your young child as actual experience.

Plant Seeds of Kindness: Fairy Tales

For thousands of years, fairy tales like "Little Red Riding Hood" have been told around the campfire to entertain children and adults. More than mere entertainment, these little stories teach life lessons like courage, honesty, and not talking to strangers (or "wolves"). The enormous popularity of these stories in every human culture on Earth testifies to their effectiveness.

With *The Happiest Toddler* version of fairy tales, you create your own special stories tailored to your child's particular needs.

What It Is: Making up stories to teach our children lessons about right and wrong and good and bad. Think of it as planting seeds of character and kindness that slowly take root in your child's spirit. It is no exaggeration to say that for young children *hearing* is believing.

Best Used For: Kids over 24 months. They love them because they're so much fun.

How It Works: When I teach parents about fairy tales, they're often afraid that they won't know what to say. Please don't worry. Think of what you want to teach your child—for example, a lesson about not getting upset when you have to go off to work every day, then use this simple three-step recipe to cook up a great fairy tale. Just think about the beginning, the middle, and the happy ending.

Telling the Tale

The Beginning: "Once Upon a Time"

Your goal at the beginning of a story is to capture your child's imagination . . . with lots of description. Start out by saying a few sentences about what the little animal hero of your story is doing and feeling (think of both her emotional feelings *and* her five-senses feelings).

> *What does the pony princess see, smell, wear, sing, eat for lunch?*
> *How does the sun feel on her face? How do the flowers smell?*
> *Is she happy, sad, curious, silly?*
> *What does she see on her walk home from school?*

Within a minute, your tot will start feeling snuggly and interested and her mind's trusting *side door* will swing open.

The Middle: "But Then"

Now weave in a little lesson about a specific behavior or value that you want your child to learn—sharing, helping others, telling the truth, saying thank you, et cetera. This is where you introduce the "problem" that has to get resolved by the end.

> But then, when she got home from school, the
> little pony wouldn't take turns; or told her
> mommy she washed her hands . . . but she hadn't;
> or teased her baby brother till he cried, etc.

> Why did she do it?
> How did her mommy feel about it?
> What did her mommy say or do (remember
> to use some of your Fast-Food Rule and Toddler-
> ese at this part).
> What did the little pony finally do that made
> her mom happy?

The End: "Happily Ever After"

Toddlers love happy endings, so always finish your stories with the problem being solved, the animals being safe, and everyone living "happily ever after."

> . . . And then the princess came home safe to
> hugs, kisses, and her favorite macaroni and
> cheese and broccoli for supper. And everyone
> lived happily ever after!

Tips to Make You a Star Storyteller:
- **Make the main characters happy little animals.**
  Pick names like Steven the Mouse or Mimi the
  Moose. Don't use children as characters. They may
  seem too real for the under-five set.

- **Tell stories where the weak triumph over the strong.** Kids love the three little pigs defeating the wolf or Jack outsmarting the giant because the little, weak guys win in the end.
- **Be a ham!** Embellish your story with whispers, funny voices, dramatic faces, and some waves of your hands to keep your child's attention.
- **If your child is more verbal, ask for suggestions.** While you tell the story, ask: "And what do you think she said then? Why do you think he was mad?"
- **Have fun adding little "helpers."** Kids love angels, fairies, talking toads, or friendly trees who come to the hero's rescue.
- **Include an animal who is grouchy and mean (but not too scary).** Include some characters who are a little ill-mannered and have them keep messing up (like "boobs") but they ultimately learn how to behave and become the hero's friend.
- **Toss in lots of special words.** Toddlers love words like "party," "secret," "castle," "princess," "superhero," "flying," "magic," "presents," "toys," "surprise," etc.

One mother shared the fairy tale she made up to help her toddler have less trouble separating from her in the mornings when she had to go to work:

> "Once upon a time there was a little girl froggie named Hoppy. She was as green as peas and loved to eat cereal for breakfast with crunchy flies in it!
>
> "Poor little Hoppy was worried every time her mommy hopped off the lily pad to go to work. But she had a talking teddy bear, and

whenever she got sad she cuddled him tight and
they would sing her favorite song together ('Old
MacDonald'!) . . . and play house . . . and
sometimes even have a tea party!

"That helped Hoppy be happy. She was also
happy when she put her hand in her pocket and
touched the magic handkerchief that her mom
gave her to help her smile when she was sad.

"Then, before she knew it, her mommy always
always always came hopping back home to the
lily pad with kisses and lots of yummy, sweet,
crunchy flies to eat . . . and they all lived happily
ever after. . . . The end!"

Plant Seeds of Kindness: Catching *Others* Being Good

Another "side-door" way to teach your child good behaviors is to comment when you see other kids (and adults) doing them. I call this **catching others being good.**

You will have many chances to use this skill. When you're driving you can comment on how nicely the drivers wait at the red light . . . or take turns at the stop sign. At stores, notice how people buy yummy food but keep it closed until they get home. At school, notice how the big kids eat with forks or how they rub their hands really hard when they wash them.

This is not a big lecture, just some casual comments on things you see people doing in books and magazines. Parenting magazines are chock-full of photos of kids doing nice things . . . and bad things. (You can use this same technique to talk about behaviors you *don't* like too.)

Later that day, let your child overhear you whispering to Daddy about what you saw and about how it makes you feel: "We saw a lot of people waiting quietly at the bank. I like it when people don't keep pushing me when I am on line."

You know you're really succeeding when your child wants you to tell her more of the adventures of the characters you've created. (So do try to remember what you say!) Story by story, you will be creating a beloved childhood memory.

Plant Seeds of Kindness: Role-Playing

> *"Pretend you're the mommy and I'm the little kid. . . ."*

Around your child's second birthday he'll start having his toys engage in little conversations and he'll like pretending to be other people (or things)—Batman, a truck, a talking duck. **Role-playing** is a way to use these fun activities to plant more seeds of kindness through the "side door" of his mind.

What It Is: In role-playing, you and your child act out a situation (or use dolls to act out situations). Role-playing is great because there's no pressure. Kids get to be silly, make mistakes, and have fun, even as they are learning.

Like actors who practice a lot to learn their lines, the more you role-play important life lessons with your child, the faster he'll learn what is right and wrong and remember it and do it in the future.

Best Used For: Children around two to three years of age. That's the time they become interested in pretending to be other people. (You can role-play with younger toddlers too, but you will have to play all the parts.)

How to Do It: As with fairy tales, you want your story to have a beginning, middle, and end to make it interesting.

But besides that basic rule, you can create endless variations on role-playing and use anything that comes to mind.

Extra Tips for Role-Playing Fun:

- **Old stories:** Act out a familiar book or fairy tale.
- **New stories:** Make up a story based on an experience that you or your child just had: someone who wasn't nice; a friend who refused to share; a little boy who wouldn't get dressed.
- **Puppet show:** If your child is too young, or too shy, to play a role, pick up a couple of dolls (puppets work well too) and use them to play the parts. For example:

> *Dog (Mom in doggie voice):* "Hey, Giraffe, I don't like it when you take my toys. You always grab and I say, 'No! No!' But when you say 'please' I am HAPPY!"
>
> *Giraffe (Mom in giraffe voice):* "Oopsie! I mean pleeeease can I play with the ball?"
>
> *Dog (Mom in doggie voice):* "You said 'please'! YEA! I like it when you say 'please'.... Okay, here it is. Can I play with one of your toys too? Please."

- **Use gossiping:** Have the dolls whisper back and forth (loud enough for your child to "overhear"). Make them talk about the behaviors that you want to encourage or discourage. (*"Hey, Mr. Teddy, did you see Mommy's face when Marley picked up her toys as quick as a bunny? Mommy was really happy and smiled big . . . like this!"*)

Don't look at your child while you gossip; it may make her suspicious that you are trying to manipulate her. Even though gossiping is done in a whisper, kids get the message loud and clear through the wide-open "side door" of their minds.

■ **Make a doll act like a boob.** It's easy to teach your lesson—and entertain your tot at the same time—if you have his doll act like a boob (confused, weak, silly, wrong, etc.).

> *"Hi! I'm Mr. Teddy, and I'm the smartest bear in the whole, entire, big, huge world! And I can walk in the street anytime I want!" Then have him pretend to walk in the street and have a little toy car screech out and knock him down.*

Here's how one dad used a minute of role-playing to teach his two-and-a-half-year-old the importance of hand washing—and prevent thirty minutes of struggle:

> *"One day before lunch, Jack and I were engaged in our usual battle over hand washing and I suddenly got the idea to see whether he might cooperate better if the hygiene advice came from his stuffed toy, Magic Bunny, instead of me. So I said, 'Wait, Jack, wait! I need to ask Magic Bunny something.' Then, I loudly whispered, 'Hi, Magic Bunny, please help us. Lunch is ready and I said "Jack, let's wash hands," and he said "No way!" and I said "Okay, let's ask Magic Bunny." So, Magic Bunny, what do you think? Should Jack wash his hands?'*
>
> *"Then I put my ear near the bunny's lips, pretending to strain to hear his response. 'What?*

What did you say? Oh . . . sure . . . okay. He
should wash his hands, but then he should give
me five . . . really hard? Okay!'

"Jack watched me, fascinated. I nodded my
head and continued, 'But can he do it fast? He
wants to eat now? Okay, Magic Bunny, I'll tell
him. Thanks! I love you, too!'

"Then I turned to my son and relayed the
message. 'Hey, Jack, Magic Bunny said he wants
you to wash your hands SUPERfast and then
give me five . . . really hard! Then we can eat
some yummy-licious food.'

"My son complied, and after lunch I gossiped
to Magic Bunny about what a great job Jack did."

Now that you're becoming an expert at flashing a green light
to signal all-systems-GO to good behavior, you're well on
your way to having fewer problems. But there will always be
some problems. And in Chapter 6 I'll discuss simple, effective
ways to flash a yellow warning light to discourage the annoying things your toddler does.

6

Yellow-Light
Behaviors:
How to Curb
Annoying Behavior

*"You can catch more flies with honey than
with vinegar."*

—Old adage

Main Points:

- Yellow-light behaviors are annoying things kids do,
  like whining, pestering, and dawdling.

- You can curb your toddler's yellow-light behaviors
  with four smart parenting skills:

  1. **Connect with Respect:** Using the Fast-Food Rule
     and Toddler-ese (plus a few other tricks) to help
     you detour around potential conflicts.

  2. **Make Your Limits Clear and Consistent:** Easy
     ways to help your child know when you *mean
     business.*

3. **Forge Win-Win Compromises:** Using your toddler's sense of fairness (and a little smart bargaining) to turn a *won't-won't* into a *win-win* . . . so both you and your child can feel triumphant.

4. **Enforce Mild Consequences: Clap-growl warnings** and **kind ignoring** are two persua-

---

The Terrible *Almost*-Twos and Tantrummy Threes

Toddlers are fun with a capital *F*! They're lively, silly, and curious. But by 18 months an unmistakable shift occurs; they become more demanding, rigid, and aggressive.

No wonder a common question doctors hear at the two-year checkup is "How bad are the terrible twos going to be?" Nervous parents who have just narrowly survived the 18-month struggles worry, *Is this going to get even harder?*

Fortunately, a toddler's *screaming meanies* usually peak at 18 months. By the second birthday the "terrible twos" are almost over.

But even if your child is past his second birthday . . . don't break out the champagne just yet. Shortly after the *third* birthday, many kids have a spurt of demanding, disrespectful behavior—the "tantrummy threes."

Interestingly, older toddlers (three to four years of age) have a lot in common with . . . tumultuous teens. Teens get *emotional whiplash* as they swing between wanting adult rights ("Everyone else can stay out late!") and reverting to childish irresponsibility ("I hate cleaning my room!"). Similarly, older toddlers swing between demanding the rights of "big kids" ("Let *me* do it!") and clinging to infantile excuses ("No, it's yucky!").

Your upset toddler is as much the victim of his intensity and immaturity as you are. But the skills I teach in this chapter will help you discourage his yellow-light behaviors . . . fast!

---

sive ways to show your child that annoying behaviors are a dead-end street.

Yellow-Light Behaviors: Annoying Little Things Your Child Says and Does

In the next chapter, I'll teach you how to put the kibosh on really bad (red-light) behaviors. But in this chapter we'll be talking about the dozens of toddler shenanigans that are not
terrible . . . just terribly annoying. These are the yellow-light
behaviors: whining, begging, clinging, pouting, interrupting,
teasing, dawdling, grabbing, yanking, screeching, fussing, and
mild defiance, to name *a few*!

Like a tiny pebble in your shoe, yellow-light behaviors can
bug the heck out of you, especially if you are tired or stressed.
Your child's annoying and defiant behavior may call up bad
memories from your own childhood, causing you to overreact and your temper to flare.

Fortunately, the four simple skills mentioned above can
quickly turn these minor conflicts back into cooperation. Study
them well. I predict you'll use them daily for years to come.

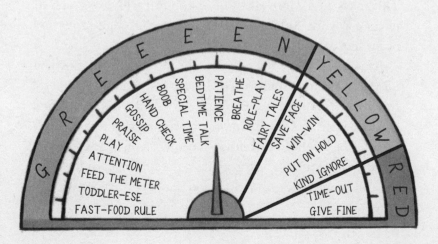

It's not just what you say, it's how you say it.

Many parents, wanting put a quick end to their child's whining and defiance, try to stop their behavior with:

- distraction—"Hey, look at this!"
- ridicule—"Don't be such a baby!"
- threats—"Stop now or I will stop you!"
- yelling—"*Stooooop!*"

While these responses may seem like the fastest way to stop the nagging, they can often backfire and quickly escalate the fight from whining to screaming, spitting, and scratching.

Like the mom and dad in the next cartoon, we all want to reach the *treasure chest of good behavior* as fast as possible. But parents who think they can go straight for it risk falling right off the cliff. *Splat!* We can all have well-behaved, respectful children, but the only sure way of achieving that is to stay on the path of good parenting. This takes a bit more effort at first, but it will save you tons of time as your child's yellow-light behaviors end faster and occur less often.

As you can see in the cartoon, the journey to good behavior starts with two skills you've already learned: the Fast-Food Rule and Toddler-ese. Echoing your child's feelings (using the Fast-Food Rule) with short phrases, repetition, and mirroring (the essence of Toddler-ese) often ends annoying behavior fast because it acknowledges the *underlying* reason for the child's misbehavior: frustration, fatigue, disappointment, boredom, etc.

What It Is: Connecting with respect means using the Fast-Food Rule + Toddler-ese (Chapters 3 and 4) to show your child that you can see the world from her perspective and you really care about her feelings. Then, once she starts to settle, it's your turn to respectfully redirect her (by offering options, distracting, giving what she wants in fantasy, etc.).

Best Used For: Any age toddler.

How to Do It: Get a little *below* your child's eye level, to show respect, and use the Fast-Food Rule + Toddler-ese. If you're not sure what to say, just use one of these easy tricks (first described on page 76):

■ **Be her "spokesperson"**—say what you think she would if she could:

> Helen was busy cooking dinner when her two-year-old, Janie, came into the kitchen, dolls in tow, wanting her mom to play. Helen sweetly told her, "Not right now, honey, Mommy is making dinner." But Janie was persistent and kept yanking on her mother's dress. So Helen acted like Janie's spokesperson:
> "Janie says, 'I'm mad . . . mad . . . mad!' She says, 'Play with me *now*!' She says, 'I want to play dolls with Mommy!' "

■ **Be her "sportscaster"**—narrate what you see:

> Had she wanted to, instead of speaking Janie's words, Helen could have chosen the sportscaster technique:
> "Janie's brought her doll to Mommy. Her face is sad and she keeps pulling and pulling on Mommy's dress!"

Key Point: Janie's mom does not *start* by saying "No!" or "Stop!" (even if it's what she's thinking). That would be like the fast-food order-taker blurting out, "Five dollars, drive up front" instead of first repeating the customer's order.

Once your child starts to calm a bit, then it's *your* turn.

As soon as Janie stopped pulling on her dress, Helen said, "Good stopping, honey. I know you want to play now, now, now! But I have to make dinner superfast, first. So you bring all your dolls and put them right here on your little table. Then, after dinner, we'll have fun playing dolls together."

You say, "No, no, <u>no</u>!" You say, "I'm <u>mad</u>!" Go away, Mommy!

Once your child starts to calm, it's your turn. There are several things you can do to help her get happy again or tell her what you need her to learn.

Offer Options. Kids love to choose. So if your child is insisting on using a breakable glass you might say, "No glass! No glass, sweetheart. Let's get one of your cool superhero cups. Which one has more supermojo, Spider-Man or Batman?"

If whining is a problem, you might say to your three-year-old, "Hillary says, 'Mommy *listen . . . now!*' I know you want Mommy to listen, sweetheart. So, do you want to use your big-girl voice or a baby voice? You pick. But my ears can't listen to that yucky whining voice. It's too yucky."

Give your tot many chances a day to pick what she wants and she'll give in much faster when you want her to go along with *your* choice.

Give Her What She Wants *in Fantasy*. When your tot can't get what she wants, at least spend a minute *pretending* she could (see the cartoon on page 54). For example, if your three-year-old is whining for a doll in a store, say, "You l-o-v-e those dolls! I wish I could give you *a hundred* of them. One hundred dolls would be sooo much fun! We could cover your whole bed with them! Which ones would you pick? Would you give some to your friends, too?"

This may sound like a tease, but it's not at all. It's a fantastic way to make your child feel heard. Remember, more than anything in the world—including those dolls—your child wants your respect, love, and caring. Your willingness to play this little game is a huge consolation prize to her: I can't really give you what you want, but I *can* give it to you in *fantasy*. It will go a long way toward comforting her even though she doesn't actually get the thing she craves.

Share Your Feelings with "You-I" Sentences. Once the dust settles, *briefly* share your feelings with a "you-I" sentence (discussed on page 54). That will help boost your child's ability to see things from *your* point of view. For example, frown, shake your head, and say, "When Sally throws flowers on the floor, it makes Mommy sad . . . sad. Mommy says, 'No hurt the flowers!' "

Offer a Distraction. After using the Fast-Food Rule + Toddler-ese, acknowledging your child's feelings, help her focus on something else.

> Maisy, 18 months, toddled over to the bookcase and began flinging books off the shelf. Her dad, Bryan, said, "No! That's not nice!" Maisy looked right at him, smiled, then knocked a few more to the floor.
>
> Bryan was tempted to yell, "No! No!" (the way his dad used to do), but then he remembered connecting with respect. So, in excited Toddlerese he bubbled, "You want book! Books! Books!!" Maisy paused and Bryan continued. "You want books! Books!!!" Then as she began to quiet, he said, "But noooo! Be gentle! No throw! No throw!" Then Bryan offered a little distraction. His eyes widened with excitement and he whispered, "Psst! Hey, come quick! I have a special book we can read together! It's FUN! It has a pussycat in it!"

Teach Values. When a three-year-old took a ball from her little sister and made her cry, her mother narrated back to the older girl her desire to take the ball, but then asked, lovingly: "Did you want to make your sister cry? Is that the kind of person you want to be?" The little girl shook her head "no." And the mother continued, "Can you think of a way to make her happy?" The toddler returned the ball and the mom told her, "Hmmm. That was a good idea. That was exactly what she wanted to be happy!"

Use Words of Criticism as "Reverse Praise." Praise tells your child the behavior you like. Criticism points out what you dislike, and it's like *reverse praise* because it uses the same rules you learned for giving your child compliments and encouragement:

- Criticize the behavior, not the child. Say, "No picking flowers" rather than "Bad boy."
- Teach your child the results of his behavior: "Chasing the dog makes him scared and mad, and he might bite."
- Gossip your disapproval to a stuffed animal or to Grandma on the phone. Gossiping dramatically boosts the attention your little one pays to your criticism:

> *Jessica hated it when her 3-year-old shoved her 9-month-old, Camille, and then refused to apologize. It was futile trying to make Lucy say she was sorry. So instead, as soon as Lucy pushed Camille, Jessica would turn her back on Lucy and gossip to Camille (loud enough so her big sister could hear): "It makes you sad when Lucy pushes you," Jessica said. "You say, 'Pushing hurts! I don't like it!' But if Sister says she's sorry, it will make Mommy very, very happy!"*

Amazingly, Lucy began to say she was sorry.
And when she did, Jessica would immediately
turn to Lucy and quietly say, "Hey, nice
apology, honey. Thanks." Then she would turn
to Camille and whisper, "Camille, did you hear?
Lucy said she's sorry. Yea, Lucy! I *like* that."

Finally, Jessica would toss out a tiny reward
to both of them and chirp, "Hey, come on,
everybody, let's go get some lemonade!"

When little Melodie kept forgetting to put
her socks in the hamper, her mom, Marta,
showed her how to make the dirty socks
march themselves there . . . and jump in.

Rick uses a "camp counselor" voice to avoid
whining and delays when it's time for his
three-year-old twins, Bethany and Brittany,
to prepare for bed. "Okay, all you rugrats,"
he says enthusiastically, "it's time for the
thrillin', chillin' pajama race! Racers' pj's on
in one minute. . . . Start your engines! On
your marks, get set, GO! Rrrrrrrrrrrrr!"

Keep It Positive

You can often avoid power struggles with one simple trick:
Tell your child what *to* do, rather than what *not* to do. For
example, "Chairs are for sitting" rather than "Stop standing
on the chair." Or "Slow down, now!" versus "Don't run!"
Or "You usually keep your feet off the new sofa, but I guess
today you forgot." Correcting behavior with positive statements makes kids feel more respected.

Another way to keep it positive is to be a little playful. For the child who is dawdling when you need to rush, try whispering what you want her to do or challenge her to a race to see who can get shoes on fastest. (During the race, play the boob by repeatedly dropping your shoes, so your child can win.) A fun way to help a child who has trouble making transitions is to make a trumpet sound to announce what's coming next.

Once you start thinking about how to get your message across effectively, you'll probably come up with dozens more ways that will make your rules seem more like play than like orders.

Sandwich your demands *between* two fun activities. For example, say, "Let's play with your trains. After that we can pick up your toys. Then it'll be time for a snack! What yummy-licious food should we eat for snack today?"

Role-Play or Tell a Fairy Tale to Illustrate Good Behavior. The technique of **planting seeds of kindness** through the side door of your child's mind can also be used to curb annoying behaviors by teaching your tot a better way to act. Here's an example of how to use a little fairy tale to teach manners:

> *Once upon a time, there was a really smart piggy princess, Penelope the pig. She loved to wear pink sneakers and to eat toast with cinnamon and sugar for breakfast. But whenever she wanted something, the little piggy always whined and hurt everyone's ears, so much that Mommy Pig had to put cotton in her ears and a big hat on her head so her ears wouldn't hurt from the little princess's sharp, whiny voice. [Imitate the whiny voice.]*

Then one day, the little piggy's friend, Betty the bunny, taught her how to use a quiet-as-a-bunny voice when she wanted to ask for something. She said, "Penelope, try it this way and everyone will like the way you sound!" [Imitate the nice voice.] Penelope tried it that very day when she wanted to go outdoors—and it worked. Even though Penelope still didn't get *everything* she wanted every time she asked, Mommy Pig was so happy that Penelope had learned a nice bunny voice that she took her to the park and they played her favorite piggy game—rolling in the mud—and they lived happily ever after.

When Roarke, a proud little three-year-old, threw cards on the floor for the tenth time that morning, his mom, Amy, demanded, "Pick them up!" Roarke pleaded for help, but Amy refused. "You threw them. You pick them up." Roarke begged, "No! I can't! It's not fair! I need help!"

Now Amy had an escalating battle on her hands. But fortunately, she knew the way out. Amy saw that Roarke had "painted himself into a corner," so rather than confronting him with threats, she offered him a few words of understanding and a compromise: "You're mad! You *hate* picking cards up by yourself. You say, 'Please help. P-l-e-a-s-e!' You threw them, but you want me to help. Hmmm, okay, if you pick up the first one, I'll pick up, hmmm, how many? Two? Three? How many do you think I should pick up?"

By Roarke's fifth birthday, Amy can expect much more responsible behavior from him. But during the toddler years, her wise goal is to respectfully validate his feelings while reminding him that he's expected to make a few baby steps of cooperation.

The connect-with-respect approach will stop many, many irksome behaviors. But, if it's not doing the trick, try offering a **win-win compromise.** (Of course, if your tot's actions or attitude are *totally* bugging you, you can immediately administer a **mild consequence;** see page 175.)

The Ancient Art of Saving Face

Have you ever heard the term "saving face"? Here "face" means "self-respect." Saving face means allowing someone to keep his dignity, even when he doesn't get his way.

Ambassadors know that shaming and disrespect are so tough to take that they can even trigger a war! That's why master diplomats *always* help their opponents *save face.* They know that allowing dignity in defeat is important because it builds forgiveness and friendship.

Saving face is important to all of us, but it is super-important to *primitive peoples* like our upset toddlers!

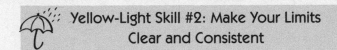 Yellow-Light Skill #2: Make Your Limits Clear and Consistent

Your first job as a parent is to give your child love, food, and shelter. But the instant she starts toddling, a new task falls on your shoulders: *limit setting.*

Limits teach toddlers the difference between right and wrong, politeness and rudeness, safety and danger, and so on. In essence, they're the walls that you will use to guide your toddler down the path of life. You may be a parent who sets up strict limits (like very close walls) or loose limits (like walls that are far apart). But once you set the rules, don't expect your tot to immediately obey all of them. While your job is to *set* limits, your little friend's job is to *push* the walls (your limits) to see if you really mean them.

If you're consistent, your tot will soon give up and go along with your demands. But mushy limits often backfire and make kids defy us even more. They push until the "wall" topples over (in other words, we give in) or until the "wall" stops moving (we hold firm).

Setting clear limits is superimportant. You must raise your children with humility and kindness, but you also need courage and resolve. Your family is *not* a democracy! Start each new day with love, but don't cave in on important limits. When push comes to shove (and shove to bite), you must respectfully use your power to keep order.

Here are four tips for effective limit setting:

1. **Be reasonable.** Unrealistic expectations are a recipe for frustration. Remember, toddlers have limited impulse control, so remove dangers and temptations (like fragile items) and make your home fit your child, rather than vice versa.

2. **Set limits with a KISS (Keep it short and simple!).** Long sentences ("Debbie, come here, please. It's time to put your crayons away. I don't want to have to ask you again. Please don't make me nag.") are too tough for your toddler's immature left brain. Simple statements work better ("Crayons stay in the den.").

3. **Be consistent.** Consistency helps kids learn a clear sense of right and wrong. Of course, no one is 100 percent consistent. There will be times when you forget or get too busy to enforce a limit. Also, there will be times when your child is whinier than usual (because of being over-hungry, tired, sick, or having a tough day), and you will choose to bend the rules. But when you do break your own rules you should clearly state that you're making a temporary exception. ("You know the rule, we only eat in the kitchen. But today is special . . . it's Daddy's birth-

day! So let's have a picnic in the living room. It will be fun, but we can only eat on the blanket.")

4. **Avoid mixed messages.** Speaking too sweetly or smiling while you set a limit confuses kids. It unintentionally gives a green light to your toddler's annoying acts. If you want your child to know you mean business, crouch down (staying just a bit *above* your child's eye level) and give your message with a deep voice and a serious face.

Pick Limits You Can Enforce

Some limits are hard to enforce. For example, it may be impossible to make a child eat broccoli, poop on the potty, or overcome fears. Picking battles you can't win may challenge your child to be *more* rebellious (*"You can't make me!"*). So when you sense you're getting into a struggle that you can't win, it's time to switch from giving warnings to using some good old charm, compromise, and ingenuity (discussed later in the chapter).

In truth, a bit of defiance is not so bad! Most parents want their kids to learn that being tenacious in their beliefs and skilled in their ability to persuade others is a good thing.

Yellow-Light Skill #3: Forging Win-Win Compromises

Turning a won't-won't into a win-win.

We're often told we should force our kids to obey. Sure, you *are* bigger and stronger, but trying to *crush* your child's acts of defiance can backfire, stunting her confidence or triggering her desire for *revenge*. Please remember, parental bullying is not a *win-win*—it's a *lose-lose*. Your child loses dignity and you hurt your relationship.

Your ultimate goal as a parent is not to win any one particular fight or another, but rather to win your child's love and respect for a lifetime. That's why, even when you disagree with her, it's best to acknowledge your tot's desire and then try to find a way you *both* can win!

In fact, even toddlers know that fairness is a two-way street: *You want* this? *Then give me* that! That's why little kids love win-win deals.

Sound hard? Actually, it's pretty easy . . . and fun!

Baby Steps—Finding a Good Compromise . . . One Step at a Time

Toddlers have trouble with giant leaps, but they're great at baby steps.

If you get into fights over tooth brushing, for example, you'll be much more successful if you break your goal into some smaller baby steps. For example, consider it a tiny success when your child lets you touch the toothbrush to his lips or teeth. Cheer, "Yea! All done. Gimme five! Let's go read some fun books!" Promptly reward this mini-cooperation with a quick dollop of fun. (I know you can't do a good cleaning in a second, but that's okay. It's a good baby step of progress.)

Over a few days, gradually increase the time you are touching to a fast count of three, and within days you'll be able to brush the teeth for a few seconds. Your next baby step is to increase the brushing to several seconds. Always end with a cheer and a little reward of fun ("feeding the meter").

But what if your toddler won't let you get a brush anywhere near his mouth? Don't fight! This is *not* a battle you can win. Instead, take even *smaller* baby steps and connect with respect. Aim for his "sweet spot" so he knows you really get his message: "*No* mouth . . . *no* mouth!" And throw in some playing the boob. "Okay, you win! You always win! No more brush. Let's get pj's on. Oh, wait! I forgot. I have to brush your knee really fast. Let's count: One, two! All done! Uh-oh . . . silly Mommy, I forgot. I have to brush your foot superfast too." (Throw in some extra boob fun by searching around for his foot in his pockets, asking, "Hey, where's your foot? Pleeease, help me find your foot!") Then, when you're finished, cheer, "Yea! All done! Let's read a book."

Now—this is important—practice this a few times every day, adding new baby steps little by little. "Okay, now the other knee. Now we brush this arm. Oh yeah, and that arm. And fingers. Now your thumb. Where's your thumb? Other thumb. Ear. Other ear." Briefly touch the brush to each place. Then say, "Yea! All done! Gimme a hard five!" And play the boob by howling and hopping in pretend pain when he does it. Within a week or two, you'll be doing some top-notch tooth brushing!

Win-win compromise is one of the top tools in this book. You'll use it again and again during the toddler years—and beyond.

All over the world, people hash out agreements by hard bargaining. Haggling over a price feels foreign to many Americans—we like straight talk—but toddlers *love* to negotiate. (Many of them could bargain the pants off a used-car salesman!) They are naturally good at bargaining tactics like begging ("Please? P-l-e-a-s-e!!!!"), exaggeration ("You *never* let me!"), pouty protests ("You're not fair!"), and noticing inconsistency ("But you let *her* do it!").

And they use these tools of persuasion to get what they want . . . every single day.

Whoa, you might be thinking, *doesn't compromising mean caving in or spoiling my child? Shouldn't I demand obedience?*

Of course, *always* giving in could spoil a child. But *demanding* obedience—"Because I say so!"—actually ends up teaching kids bad lessons (*what you think is unimportant* and *might makes right*). On the other hand, finding reasonable compromises teaches kids to be more fair and flexible.

Remember, you're strong and smart and your toddler is weak, short, slow, and can't speak very well. So he feels like he is losing over and over and over again. Win-win compromises will teach him that both you *and* he can be winners, that people who love each other can each give in *a bit* and still be strong.

If you want your child to grow up fair-minded and respectful, the best way to teach him is by *your* example.

What It Is: Finding a win-win compromise is a big part of the ancient art of negotiating: "I'll trade you one of these for two of those." It shows fairness, respect, and good listening. Most kids do this automatically, from a one-year-old trading kisses to a teenager negotiating for a bigger allowance.

Win-win compromises give kids practice at being fair and teach them that solutions can be found that allow both parties to give in a little without losing dignity.

Some parents ask, "Why should I compromise? I give my child plenty! She isn't running the show!" You're correct to expect your child to be more grateful by five or six. But younger children have not yet mastered the fine points of civilization, like appreciating someone's generosity . . . especially when they're upset. (Even many adults have trouble with *that*!)

Best Used For: Toddlers age two and up.

The 90-10 Compromise: Your Toddler's Idea of What's Fair

We all want to be treated fairly . . . especially toddlers! They can deal with frustrations and demands much better when they feel like they're getting a fair deal. (On the other hand, unfair treatment can make resentment harden into bitter memories and ruin relationships.)

But who's to say what is fair?

Most grown-ups consider a 50-50 compromise to be pretty fair: half for you, half for me. But that's not the way your toddler sees things. His idea of a reasonable compromise is probably around 90-10. (You get a tiny piece and he gets the *90* percent!)

Now, this may sound unfair to you, but take a moment to see things through your little friend's eyes and you'll see that for him an even split feels terrible. That's because toddlers tend to focus on what they *don't* get. *(Hey, I want that, too!)* Their primitive, cave-kid minds are kind of greedy and have trouble sharing.

Clever parents know that if they let their tot win many "small" struggles (things they really don't care about), their kids give in more easily on the issues they do care about.

Of course, there are some situations where you will not be able to compromise—situations that involve danger, aggression, or important family rules. But you'll have fun using the win-win approach for the dozens of situations each day when you *can* compromise.

At first your compromises will be 90-10 in your toddler's favor. But, once you've used this system for a while, you'll gradually teach him that sometimes he has to give in more. As he grows older, you'll get him to make 70-30 deals . . . and eventually even 50-50 compromises.

How to Do It: The win-win technique can be boiled down to three easy steps:

Step 1. Connect with respect. Use the FFR + Toddlerese to acknowledge what your child wants.

Step 2. Make a "crummy" offer. Offer a 90-10 compromise (where *you* get 90 percent and your child gets only 10 percent of what she wants).

> You offer a "bad deal" so your tot can immediately reject it. Sound odd? It's actually one of the oldest bargaining tricks in the world! You make an offer you're prepared to allow her to reject so that she can feel like a tough negotiator, like she's driving a *hard bargain*.

Step 3. "Reluctantly" give in. When she refuses, come back with an offer that gives her *most* of what she wants . . . she gets 90 percent and you get 10 percent.

Act like she's the toughest negotiator you've ever seen. Pretend to be a bit reluctant to agree ("Okay . . . okay . . . it's not fair, but I guess you win."). This makes your child feel like a *winner*—like she's getting the best deal possible. (Ham it up a little!)

Imagine you want your child, Sam, to eat ten peas and he refuses, demanding instead his favorite crackers. Here's how you might put the 90-10 compromise idea into action:

Step 1. Connect with respect: "Sammy says, 'No, *no*! No peas!' Sammy says 'no peas!' Sammy wants crackers!"

Step 2. Make a "crummy" offer: Remove two peas from the plate but keep eight in front of him and say,

"Okay, okay. You win! You can have crackers, but first you have to eat this many peas. Okay? Come on, eat them up!"

Sammy turns up his nose saying, "No!"

Step 3. Now give in 90 percent . . . and seem defeated: Pout and wave your hands (as if to indicate *I give up*). Then say, "Okay! Sammy wins! Sammy wins! I *never* win! You win a *hundred* times! You say, 'No peas!' Okay! Here are your crackers. . . ." But a second after showing him the crackers, take them back and say, "Uh-oh! I forgot. First, eat just one teeny, tiny, baby pea . . . then, you get a bunch of crackers!"

All good negotiators know when to *talk* . . . and when to *walk*. If your toddler totally refuses your best offer, turn your back and ignore him for a minute before trying again.

For example, if Sammy totally refuses to eat any peas (or even to touch one!), acknowledge his refusal but then have him leave the table so that he doesn't get to eat the food he does want. This puts a pause on the negotiations—so *you* can **save face**—and helps him see that stubbornness won't get him what he wants.

"You say *no* peas! Not even *one*! That makes Mommy sad, but okay . . . you win. So no crackers for now and you go play; I'll check on you in a little bit. Bye-bye."

Speed your child's learning by giving many opportunities to compromise. For example, offer peas a few days in a row, even during lunch. Most kids will eventually accept a 90-10 deal. And, gradually, life will get easier as your tot starts to like making "win-win" deals with you.

This may seem like a big effort, but all your extra work now will soon lead to you having a happier—and fairer—child.

> Jack, age three, hated shoes and socks but loved sandals. That was okay with his mom, Shaya, on most days, but this day it was raining badly. After his mom's Toddler-ese failed to persuade him to put on shoes, Shaya offered a "crummy" 50-50 compromise: "Wear the shoes now, and you can have the sandals after school." Jack flat-out refused: "No way!"
>
> Then Shaya sat on the floor and pretended Jack was just too tough a bargainer for her. "Okay! You win! You win! You always win!" Then she offered another deal: Jack could either wear one shoe and one sandal now and put the other shoe on at school, or he could wear sandals to the car and put shoes on when the car arrived at the school. He accepted the latter and Shaya made a little pen check on his hand for being so helpful.

I find 90-10 compromises are a big help when I'm examining unhappy toddlers. For example, I start by "losing" several times in a row. With the child on his mom's lap and me kneeling just below eye level (to be a little less threatening), I beg for something he has: Putting my hand out, I plead, "Please, can I have your shoe? P-l-e-a-s-e?"

When he refuses, I continue playing the boob by sounding even more pitiful. "Okay, but can I have your teddy? Please? Pleeeease?" When he refuses again I say, "Okay! You win. You *always* win me. But what about your shirt? I really, really *need* it! Can I have your shirt? Pleeeeease?"

I usually ask for several things in succession, sulking and pouting with each rejection ("You win, you always win!"). By then, even the most reluctant child feels like a winner: safe, strong, and triumphant! (And besides, they think it's kind of funny.)

Next, I ignore the child for a minute while I talk to the parent. By this time, the child knows he's "beaten me" so many times that it's only fair to let me win a tiny bit! After a few minutes, I turn back to the child and ask for something very simple: "Can I listen to your *shoe*?" Most kids don't resist this. Then, I immediately reward the cooperation by letting him hold one of my little toys.

Put Annoying Behavior "On Hold" . . .
with Patience-Stretching

I *love* persistent kids. But, if your tenacious tyke runs over your rules like a steamroller, try this little twist on patience-stretching to put her annoying behavior on hold:

First, practice patience-stretching (page 122) several times to teach your toddler that when you hold up a finger and say, "Wait! Wait!" she has to be patient.

Now you are ready to use this great technique to discourage her pestering. For example, your child is nagging you to let her play with her ball, but you don't want her to play with it inside the house:

1. Connect with respect: Use the FFR + Toddler-ese to acknowledge her feelings.

   > *"You want! You want the ball! You say, 'Mine! Mine!! Give it to me!' You really, really want it!"*

2. Next, *almost* give her what she wants . . . but then *stop and turn away:* Reach for the ball, but then suddenly act like you need to do something important. Then ignore her for five seconds as you pretend to do something else.

   > *"Sure, honey. I'll get it. But, uh-oh! Wait! Wait! One second, one second!"*

3. Now, turn back and again *begin* to get the ball, but suddenly stop and tell her you remembered you "can't" give it to her . . . but you can offer a good compromise. It sounds like this:

   > *"Good waiting, sweetheart, here's the ball." Then, suddenly look surprised and exclaim, "But . . . wait! Wait! I almost forgot, no balls in the house . . . noooo balls. I'm so sorry, honey, but you know the rule. We can play with the ball outside or we can play with your dolls inside. Which one would you like?"*

With an older toddler, you might use a timer:

> For five miserable minutes, three-and-a-half-year-old Jackson nagged his dad to play. Craig resisted because he was making dinner. Then he remembered the tip of putting whining "on hold": "Okay, you win. You win. I'll play a tiny bit," he said. But just as Craig started to leave the stove, he put up one finger and announced, "Wait! Wait!!" as if he suddenly remembered something.
>
> He reached for the timer, set it for twenty seconds, and said, "I'm sooo sorry, Jackster! I forgot . . . I have to do one more thing. Mr. Dinger will ding really soon and then we can play and have fun!"
>
> Jackson paused his rant and waited quietly. The instant the timer went off, Craig clapped and said, "Good waiting. Now tell me what you want."
>
> "Play with me," Jackson said in a calmer tone, holding two cars in his hand.
>
> Craig chirped, "Sure, buddy." He sat down with his son, but a few seconds after starting to play Craig suddenly stopped, saying, "Oh, wait! Wait! Oh, silly Daddy, I almost forgot I have to make the salad. Just one more minute." And he got up and set the timer again.
>
> Craig briefly worked on the salad until the dinger rang again, then stopped to offer a compromise: "Good waiting. We can play for one little minute right now, or we can play for five big minutes later if you wait nicely while Daddy makes salad."

Just like the parents in the cartoon on page 151, this *long way around* will require some extra effort from you, but you'll find that over time, it will keep you from *falling off the cliff* into endless conflicts and fights.

Reverse Psychology: Get Your Child to Do Something . . . by Telling Her *Not* to Do It

From 18 months on, our little cave-kids love to defy us. It makes them feel powerful and independent. **Reverse psychology** is a playful way to take advantage of this natural tendency to rebel by telling your toddler she can't (or shouldn't) do something that you really want her to do. Then she can defy your "order" and still end up doing exactly what you *wanted* her to do in the first place. . . . Everybody wins!

For example, if your three-year-old hates kissing you, surprise her by ordering her *not* to kiss you. (Ham it up a little. . . . Don't sound serious.) Cover your face with your hands and say in a pretend-begging voice, "Pleeeease don't kiss me! No, no! Don't do it!" Then as she "defies you" to give you kisses, act unable to push her away, and complain, "Bleah . . . bleah. Yucky!" as she gleefully plants hugs and kisses all over you.

Reverse psychology doesn't teach kids to be disobedient. It's really just another way of playing the boob. Toddlers know it's a game, that's why they love it. They get to be their own boss, defy you a bit, and still end up cooperating. It's great!

Finally I ask him if I can to listen to his stomach, his knee (for another little joke), and then his heart.

The idea of negotiating with your toddler may seem odd, and of course you can't compromise on some issues (running into the street, slapping a friend, etc.). But you'll be amazed how often negotiating can smooth over the myriad minor troubles that arise in a day. And by the time your tot is a teen (and a *truly* wily opponent), you'll be a world-class expert on negotiations and finding respectful win-win compromises!

Communicating with respect, setting limits, and finding win-win compromises can stop many annoying behaviors. But if

you've done your best and your child is still defying you, it's time for you to use the next tool: **mild consequences.**

Yellow-Light Skill #4: Mild Consequences

How to deliver clear warnings . . . and mild penalties.

If all else fails and your child's yellow-light behaviors are just not stopping, it may be time for a mild consequence. Here are the two that I use the most: **clap-growl warnings** and **kind ignoring.**

Clap-Growl Warnings: Get Your Child's Attention Fast

If your toddler continues the annoying behavior even after you respectfully acknowledge her and offer an option or compromise, try clap-growl. Even a one-year-old will get the message that you're out of patience and a real penalty is coming if she doesn't stop . . . fast.

For example, if your two-year-old threatens to dump spaghetti on her head, what do you think would stop her faster: saying "No" with a big grin on your face, or frowning, clapping your hands hard, and growling, "Nooooo!"?

What It Is: All kids (even uncivilized tots) understand that a few hard claps and a low grrrrrrrrrrowl mean *"Stop . . . now . . . or you won't like what happens next!"* (Bonus: A few hard claps also help us vent a bit of anger, without resorting to spanking or yelling.)

I admit this sounds, well, undignified. But as you know by now, kids who are upset rely on their right brain, which is not good at words but is great at understanding non-verbal communication, including voice, facial expressions, and gestures. Clap-growl warnings can quickly connect with upset toddlers and often stop annoying behaviors in seconds!

Best Used For: All toddlers, starting at 9 months.

How to Do It:

Step 1: Clap. Clap your hands three to four times, hard and fast. (It's meant to be a little startling.) As you clap, you can stand or kneel, but you must remain a bit *above* your child's eye level (to emphasize your authority).

Step 2: Growl. Put a scowl on your face and make a deep, rumbling growl. If it works and your child stops quickly, immediately do a little FFR + Toddler-ese, and then feed the meter a bit (with hugging, attention, play, or playing the boob) to show you appreciate your little one's cooperation.

Warning: The first time you growl, your child may smile or even growl back! Don't worry. That may mean your growl was too *sweet* (she thinks it's a game) or she wants you to smile . . . so you won't be mad. Simply answer her growl with a couple of **double takes** (see box below) and *then* growl again.

> *"Benjamin knows I'm serious when I growl," says*
> *Claudia. "I start out with 'Gentle, gentle' or 'Use*
> *your words.' But if that doesn't work I rumble*
> *out a growl and it works immediately. He knows*
> *I'm done putting up with his behavior. I feel like*
> *a mama bear teaching her cub. In fact, now*
> *when he's mad he growls instead of biting."*

Do a Double Take to Show You're Serious

What It Is: A double take is a neat little trick that emphasizes to your child that you're not kidding around.

How to Do It: After a few seconds of clap-growling, raise a finger (as if to indicate "Wait a second") and look away for two seconds, keeping your finger up the whole time. Then, look back, growl, scowl, and repeat your message. ("No! Stop *now!*")

I recommend adding a double take to your growl if:

- Your child ignores your clap-growl.
- You and your child are stuck glaring at each other (long glaring often backfires and pushes kids to be *more* defiant).
- You want to emphasize your frustration and underscore that you are the boss.

A double take can also help if you accidentally smile while growling (even misbehaving toddlers can look so cute!). Bite your lip, hold up a warning finger, and look away for a moment—to regain your composure—then turn back and say in a serious voice, "I'm *not* happy! I say, *No!* No putting jelly in your hair."

I often use clap-growl with young children who ignore my kind requests to stop. I clap my hands hard and *g-r-o-w-l* a warning deep in my throat. That usually stops them fast . . . the way we immediately slow down when a police car's light flashes in our rearview mirror!

As your child matures, you'll growl less. But you'll probably continue clapping and/or using a silent cue like a frown, raised eyebrow, or straight index finger as a warning that your patience is up.

> "When my mom got angry with me, she would glare, raise her right eyebrow, and then hold up a warning finger. I quickly learned to stop—pronto—or else I wasn't going to like what came next."
>
> —Hillary about her mother, Mary, who raised seven kids

> When 18-month-old Aaron was about to whack his pal Tomas over a disputed toy, Aaron's mom, Joy, frowned, stomped her foot, shook her head, and growled. Then she waved her hands as if to indicate "The deal's off!" and gruffly said, "Mad! Mad!!!! Aaron mad!! Aaron says, 'No, Tomas! No truck!' Aaron mad . . . mad!!"
>
> In an instant, Aaron lowered his hand. Joy said, "No hit. Good boy! Come on, kids . . . let's get some juice!" Later in the day, when tempers cooled, Joy "gossiped" about the incident to Aaron's teddy: "Mr. Teddy, I said, 'No hit, no hit!' And Aaron stopped fast. Aaron was a very good listener!"

When your child heeds your warning, reward him right away with a smidge of attention, praise, or play. This teaches him, *You be good to me and I'll be good to you.* However, if his annoying behavior continues, it's time for a slightly stronger consequence (kind ignoring).

Kind Ignoring: Give Your Tot a Little Cold Shoulder

When your child is scared or hurt, you should do everything you can to soothe her. But there are two situations where your attention actually prolongs upsets:

- With a child whose tears keep flowing because she's in front of an audience—*the drama queen scenario.*
- With superstubborn kids who are so *proud* that they're forced to continue their protests as long as you are watching them.

In both of these situations, you need to remove the "spotlight" (your attention) and do some kind ignoring.

What It Is: Kind ignoring is giving your child a teensy *cold shoulder* to nudge her back to cooperation.

Now, when I say "ignore" I don't mean you should be rude or cruel or turn your back on really bad behavior. This type of ignoring also shouldn't be done when your child is frightened, hurt, or genuinely sad. But when you feel your child is being unreasonable and stubborn, a little kind ignoring can be perfect.

Best Used For: Toddlers of any age.

Sadie, 15 months old, found a fun thing her voice could do: screech! She blasted her new sound whenever she wanted attention. "At first we rushed right over," explained her dad, Bill. "But we soon realized that Sadie had learned to do this for any little frustration." I suggested to Bill that rather than hurrying over, he try kind ignoring.

The next day, when Sadie screeched to get a book, Bill narrated her strong feelings by jabbing

the air with his finger, pointing to the book, and
exclaiming, "You want book! Sadie wants book,
now! But no screech! Ouch! Ouch! (He covered
his ears with his hands and shook his head.)
Indoors voice, please!"

When Sadie continued screeching, Bill frowned
and continued, "You want book. Book, book,
book! But . . . ouch! Ouch! That hurts my ears! You
find your nice voice . . . and I'll be right back."

Bill turned his back briefly, pretending to be
busy. "It was amazing," he reported later. "After
ten seconds of shrieking even louder, she just
stopped and said nicely, 'Book . . . book!' And I
immediately got the book and sat down with her
to reward her for using her indoors voice."

How It's Done: Kind ignoring has three steps. You should
expect that it will take a little practice for you to get the hang
of it . . . and for your tot to realize that whining doesn't work
anymore.

Step 1: Connect with respect. Narrate her actions and
feelings like a sportscaster (don't forget to aim for
her sweet spot). "You're sad . . . sad . . . *sad*! Your
face is sad and you're *mad*! You want to jump on the
table, but Daddy said, 'No, no, *no*!' So now you're
on the floor crying."

Step 2: Lovingly turn away. If your tot continues whining, withdraw your attention with kindness. "You're
crying and *mad*! Daddy loves you *so* much, you go
ahead and cry and I'll be right back!" Then walk to

the other side of the room or sit right by your child, but pretend not to look at her.

Now act busy for twenty seconds (not so much to make her panic but enough to make your point).

Key point: As soon as your child stops the annoyance, promptly return, lovingly echo her feelings again, and then offer *your* message of reassurance, explanation, etc. Finally, feed the meter (hug, give attention, play, or play the boob) for a minute to reward her cooperation.

Step 3: Return . . . and try again. If your child continues the yellow-light behavior, return when the twenty seconds are up and repeat steps 1 and 2 a few times until your uncivilized friend starts to calm down.

If your child is particularly stubborn, her crying may persist despite several attempts at kind ignoring. In that case, turn your back for a longer time—a minute or two—until she quiets. Once she calms, return and try to engage her in some play. (Don't be surprised if she resists at first. She may need to ignore you for a few minutes to save her pride.)

If the misbehavior persists, or escalates, despite kind ignoring, you are now in a red-light situation. This requires a stronger "**take-charge**" **consequence,** like time-out, described in the next chapter.

Other behaviors that warrant a "take-charge" consequence include any actions that are dangerous or aggressive or that break an important family rule. I discuss all of these situations and how to deal with them in the next chapter.

Warning: When you first try kind ignoring the pestering may temporarily get worse before it gets better. Psychologists call this an *extinction burst.* Your child thinks, *Hmmm . . . whining always worked* before. *Maybe Mom just didn't hear me. I better follow her into the next room and yell* louder *so she hears me!* But stick with it and you'll soon see big improvements.

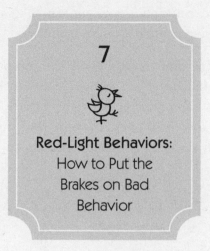

7

Red-Light Behaviors:
How to Put the
Brakes on Bad
Behavior

"Spare the discipline, spoil the child."

—T. Berry Brazelton

Main Points:

- All toddlers do "bad" things . . . sometimes.

- Acts that are dangerous or aggressive or that break important family rules are red-light behaviors.

- Red-light behaviors require prompt and clear limit setting.

- Put the brakes on your toddler's red-light deeds with a "take-charge" consequence: **time-out** or **giving a fine**.

- Time-outs work the best when started early and done exactly right.

- For older toddlers, giving a fine (losing a valued privilege or possession) is a useful penalty.

- Effective discipline does not require resorting to spanking, intimidation, or humiliation.

When we respectfully reward good acts and punish bad behaviors, our kids learn the rules . . . fast! So, now that you know how to boost good (green-light) behaviors and reduce annoying (yellow-light) ones . . . you're ready to learn how to stop the totally unacceptable (red-light) ones.

Three Red-Light Behaviors You Must Stop . . . Fast

There are three types of bad behaviors that go beyond the "annoying" category and need to be stopped in their tracks.

- **Dangerous acts:** Running into the street, grabbing hot coffee, playing with knives—any behavior that puts your child (or someone else's) in harm's way.
- **Aggression:** Hitting, spitting, kicking, biting, and other mean acts.
- **Breaking key family rules:** These are rules *you* get to choose. Some of them might fit just about all families (like no drawing on the walls), but others vary from home to home, for example, no eating in the living room, no touching the computer, no calling your brother an idiot.

All of these behaviors demand swift action, often with a "take-charge" consequence: time-out or giving a fine.

Stopping bad behaviors doesn't mean rolling up your sleeves and fighting your child mano a mano. Like the world's top ambassadors, you can stop most conflicts by establishing clear consequences in a respectful manner. So put away your boxing gloves, and read on to sharpen up your diplomatic skills.

Flash a "Red Light" on Bad Behaviors

Susan is at her wit's end. Her 18-month-old, Shane, used to be so easy. But now he gets furious when he can't have his way. "Lately Shane hits when he's mad. Distraction doesn't work anymore. I don't want to spank him, but what should I do when he looks right at me . . . and disobeys?"

If you've mastered the yellow-light techniques, but your primitive little buddy is still plowing right through the limits, you must either fix the problem that's making your child so ornery (see avoiding problem situations on page 225) or back up your words with a clear negative consequence: punishment.

Punishment is merely a negative response that tells a child when she has crossed a boundary. In truth, it's your responsibility to take control of her behavior when she is unable (too upset or too mischievous) to respect your rules. Remember, this is not something you are doing to your child; she is the one who's bringing the consequences upon herself.

Why Good Kids . . . Do Bad Things

It's hard to be good *all* the time . . . even for adults! No wonder our little tykes have days when their impulsive, primitive nature takes control and makes them do things they shouldn't. Here are some of the reasons why good kids do bad things:

- **Toddlers can't explore without testing the rules.** Your tot is an ace explorer—persistent and gutsy. His job is to touch, bang, and pull everything. That is annoying to you because it makes him constantly push the limits. However, from his point of view, you are irritating because you're trying to stop his greatest joy—discovery.
- **Toddlers are impulsive.** You can't expect an 18-month-old, or even a three-year-old, to use good judgment (like not eating medicine, or holding hands in a parking lot). Toddlers live in the "now," and their immature brains don't focus much on the consequences.

- **Our threats paint kids into a corner.** Trying to force defiant tykes to obey often backfires. Our pressure makes them feel painted into a corner, unable to give in without feeling humiliated. That's why threats often trigger *more* defiance (and hurt the relationship we work so hard to build), especially in toddlers who are temperamentally challenging and stubborn to begin with.
- **Our limits are inconsistent and confusing.** Mushy limits invite kids to push against them. (Your child thinks, *Sometimes this is allowed and sometimes not. Let's see if I can do it now.*) They get especially confused when our limits make no sense . . . to them: *What? I love jumping on the sofa more than* anything *in the world—and you want to stop me? Don't you love me anymore?*
- **Our rules are unrealistic.** Many toddlers act "bad" if our expectations are too high. Would you demand good table manners from a six-month-old? Of course not! Well, similarly, it's unrealistic to expect an 18-month-old to share, a two-year-old to never lie, or a three-year-old to sit still in church.
- **Toddlers are overexposed to aggression.** Little kids love to imitate, and that includes bad stuff like shouting and hitting. Make it your job to protect your child from seeing violence on TV, in your community, and between the members of your family.
- **Toddlers have too many stresses.** Stress can turn a *kind kid* into a *cave-kid.* When your child is acting up, ask yourself: Is my child hungry? Bored? Tired? Overloaded with rules? Sick? Teething? Surrounded by temptations? Cooped up? Wild from something in his diet (cola/chocolate/iced tea/sugar/decongestants)?

Jealous? Are there extra stresses at home (new baby, new sitter)?

- **You're giving too little play and attention.** Busy parents accidentally teach their little ones to be defiant or disrespectful by ignoring them when they are good. Thomas Gordon in his book *Parent Effectiveness Training* calls this the Law of the Soggy Potato Chip (just as kids would rather have soggy potato chips than none at all, toddlers would rather be yelled at than ignored).

When your child is engaged in red-light behaviors, there are two "take-charge" consequences you can use to put on the brakes: time-out and giving a fine. Let's look at each of them in detail. . . .

 ## Time-Out: A Parenting Classic

Time-out is a classic discipline tactic. It is *not* a sign of failure—yours or your child's. Toddlers are *supposed* to push the limits. But we need to be ready to give clear signals when they push too far.

Toddlerhood is the most dangerous period of childhood— at least until your child gets his first dirt bike! And it is *your* job to teach your tot to be careful. Time-outs train toddlers to take our words seriously and to heed our warning *before* a catastrophe occurs.

Take running away from you in a parking lot, for example. Perhaps your child dashes off the instant you start putting groceries in the trunk. Of course you'll run after him, but that may make him run even *faster* . . . thinking it's a game of chase. What you really want is a special signal that your child always listens to, one that means *Stop, now! Or you won't like what happens next.* Time-out is the way of teaching your child that your warnings must be heeded.

During the months after a child's first birthday, I recommend doing time-outs several times a week. That helps your tot learn your *I'm not kidding!* signal. Your serious tone of voice, disapproving frown, and counting to three will make him remember, *Uh-oh . . . when my mom counts like that I always get grounded. . . . I better stop!*

What It Is: **Time-out** is a "**take-charge**" **consequence** where you *very briefly* deprive your child of two precious things: freedom and the privilege of being with you.

Best Used For: All toddlers! (I advise teaching **time-outs** at the one-year checkup and strongly recommend that parents use them many times over the following months.)

How to Do It: Time-out requires one piece of equipment—a timer—and has three simple steps (Note: For dangerous or really bad behavior you can skip right to step 3):

Step 1: **One last warning.** Use clap-growl and connect with respect one last time, to get your child's attention and show that you care. If the problem stops, silently congratulate yourself—you sidestepped a conflict.

For example, if your two-year-old is having a meltdown at the dinner table because you won't let him play with the sugar bowl, clap-growl, frown, and shake your head "no" (even do a double take). Once you have his attention say, "Mad. *Mad.* Jamie's *mad* at Daddy. He's mad, mad, mad! Jamie wants the sugar, now! But . . . no sugar! *No* sugar!

But you know what? Daddy's gonna let you hold something else. Do you want to hold a piece of bread or your police car?"

Step 2: Count to three. If your child ignores your warning, put on a serious face and *calmly* echo his desire; then say "No," and count to three. (Wait one to two seconds between each number and count on your fingers too, so your child can see and hear you at the same time. "Jamie says, 'Sugar, now!' but Daddy says, 'No way.' Does Jamie want a time-out to get calm again? One . . . two . . . three . . .")

You want your child to learn that the time-out is something he's doing to himself (not something you're doing to be mean). Think of it like a sports time-out . . . a short break in the action: "I guess you want a little time to cool off."

If your child stops misbehaving before you get to three, *don't* do a time-out. Reward his cooperation with some FFR and feeding the meter with a little time-in, playing the boob, or a hand check. Later on, compliment his good listening with a bit of praise and gossip, and a little bedtime sweet talk before you turn out the lights.

Step 3: Put your child in isolation. Now the time for talking is over. Calmly lead him (or, if you have to, carry him) to the time-out place: "Come with Daddy so you can get calm again."

Twenty-two-month-old Phoebe loved her mom's fancy high-heel shoes. Several times a day she begged to put them on. But her mom, Charlene, was afraid they'd be ruined.

After learning about *The Happiest Toddler*, Charlene tried the new approach. She narrated her daughter's desire four to five times (reflecting enough of her emotion to hit the "sweet spot"). Then she offered a solution: Phoebe's choice of three other pairs of shoes. But Phoebe's eyes were locked on to her favorite ones as she wailed pitifully, "Choos! Choos!" over and over . . . and over!

After 20 seconds of connecting with respect, Charlene changed her tactic to kind ignoring. Energetically pointing to the shoes, she exclaimed, "Shoes! Shoes! You want shoes. You want shoes *now*! But Mommy says, 'No! No shoes!' So you go ahead and cry—I love you so much—and I'll be back in just a minute."

Phoebe got so mad she gave a glass-shattering shriek and started to knock things off the table. At that point, Charlene decided that Phoebe was breaking an important family rule and needed to be stopped immediately before she broke something. So she clapped her hands hard a few times to get Phoebe's attention, and said, "No throwing! No throwing!" And she carried Phoebe to her room and set the timer for an immediate time-out.

Time-Out: The Basic Rules

Does the idea of giving a time-out make you nervous? Most of us feel awkward when we do something new (like the first time we fed or bathed our baby). Here are some tips to help it go well:

Start with *Mini Time-Outs*. The first few times you use this approach just move your child to the next room.

Imagine your child is hitting the window with a toy. Say, "No! No! Windows are not for hitting. Give me the toy." If he refuses, count: "One . . . two . . . three . . ." If he still refuses, quietly take his hand and lead him to another room. Then say, "No hitting windows!" and walk away—with the door wide open.

Don't worry about making him stay put. You just want him to see that ignoring you will lead to a moment of isolation for him.

However, if he goes right back to banging the window, calmly count to three and do a regular time-out.

Pick Your Time-Out Place Ahead of Time. A chair or bottom step may work with some tots. But young ones, and feisty toddlers of all ages, usually need to be confined—in a playpen if they are under age two, or gated into their bedroom if they are over age two (see page 196).

Of course, you must make sure there are no breakables, hard surfaces, or sharp corners in the time-out place.

(Some parents choose to sit their toddlers on their laps and hold them firmly as a type of restrictive punishment. That's fine *if* it works for you. But I find that for most toddlers, especially spirited ones, this can turn the time-out into a power struggle.)

Buy a Timer with a Loud Ring. Timers are great to let both you and your child know when the time-out is over. Keep it where you can get to it quickly. Introduce the timer to your tot as Mr. Dinger and let him hear what it sounds like. Explain that Mommy will let him out of his room when Mr. Dinger goes "ring-ring."

Make the Time-Out Last One Minute per Year of Age. A time-out for your one-year-old would be one minute, two minutes for your two-year-old, etc. I recommend that you always use the timer. It allows your child to hear when the time-out is over and it also gives you a good answer when he begs to come out. ("It's not up to me, it's up to Mr. Dinger.")

When Time-Out Is Over *It's Over*! When the time's up, let your child go free. I like to ask, "Are you ready to come out now?" Even if he says "No!" I open the door, as long as he is not still tantrumming. ("Okay, you can stay if you want, but the time-out is over.") If he is still carrying on, acknowledge that he is very angry and that it sounds like he needs some extra time-out to find his calm.

Once the fit is over and your child is free to go, don't talk about the time-out for thirty minutes or so. Just join him in some play or give a bit of attention. It's time to let go of your anger and allow your heart to forgive. If *he's* still mad, connect with respect, but then let him be on his own. Many kids need to sulk a little after being punished.

> *"You hate time-out . . . you say no time-out,*
> *Mommy. I know you hate it, but Sammy needed*
> *a little help to find his calm again. Do you want a*
> *hug? No? Okay, you're still mad, mad, mad! I love*
> *you, sweetheart, and I'll check on you in a couple*
> *of minutes."*

Awhile after a time-out, express your regret for having had to do it. "Mommy knows you don't like time-out. You were *mad*. I'm sorry. Next time, I hope we can *play* instead of you needing a time-out." Later in the day, talk to him about what happened and gossip to his toys about the incident (and the lesson you want him to learn). At bedtime, reinforce the lesson by telling a fairy tale about a little bunny who misbehaved and what happened to him.

Time-Outs Don't Work Without *Time-Ins*

If time-out doesn't seem to be working, maybe it's because you haven't been giving him enough time-ins. Toddlers hate unfairness even more than they hate punishment. Ignore your child too much and he'll feel justified in defying you. On the other hand, "feed his meter" with plenty of little time-ins and playing the boob and he'll naturally be more cooperative. So if your child is getting too many time-outs, he probably needs more time-ins! (Just five minutes of time-in each hour can prevent many problems.)

What If My Child Won't Stay in His Room When I Do Time-Out?

Standing guard over the "naughty" chair or playing tug-of-war over the doorknob to keep your child in his room defeats the whole purpose of time-out—which is to ignore the child, isolating him and depriving him of your attention for a couple of minutes.

That's why, for tots under two, I recommend playpens for time-outs. And, over two, I recommend using their bedroom and blocking the door with a baby gate. However, if your child can climb over the gate, you'll need to close the door and either use a childproof doorknob cover to prevent those little hands from opening the door, or you have to lock it, using a simple hook-and-eye-type latch affixed to the outside of the door.

What? Did He Say to Lock My Child in His Room? Isn't That Cruel?

The reason for locking the time-out place is to enable you to maintain control, which is hard to do if your child can escape. However, before using a locked room for a time-out, twice a day for the next few days you should let your child see that you can lock the door so that he can no longer open it with a simple turn of the knob. Let him try to open the door from the outside and point out the locked latch. ("See, honey, the door stays closed.") Explain that it's to help him stay inside for time-outs. ("Remember when Mommy held the door closed and you were really mad? You said, 'No, no, *no!*' Now Mr. Lock will keep the door closed even when you try to open it. Mommy will open it when Mr. Dinger rings.")

Isolating your little one in his room for two minutes is neither mean nor unfair. All the love you give him the other 23 hours and 58 minutes of the day more than makes up for this short penalty! Trust me, your child can handle two minutes alone in his bedroom—his favorite room of the house. (Of course, *never* use a closet, bathroom, basement, or non-childproofed space for time-out.)

Time-Out: Advanced Rules

Now that you know the basics, here are a few extra tips:

Don't Say Much. This is superimportant! Once you start counting, stay calm and neutral. The less you say, the more your child's stressed-out brain will be able to hear. The time for your explanations and being friends again will come later . . . after time-out is over.

Don't Be Emotional. Adults who get upset when they do time-outs may make kids protest and fight even more. *Our* emotional reaction can accidentally backfire and make our uncivilized little friends feel "challenged to fight," causing them to respond with the primitive fury of tiny Neanderthals.

Do Time-Out the Same Way Every Time. Consistency helps kids learn. Use the same tone of voice, stern face, and counting speed each time. Pretty soon, your tot will recognize exactly when you're serious and *give in* before you get to three.

> *Molly found that after doing time-outs about ten times, her 15-month-old Albert stopped pushing the limits so much. She found that just raising her warning finger and sternly saying, "One!" usually made him stop, so that he rarely needed time-outs anymore.*

Don't Wait Too Long. The best time to teach discipline is right when the misbehavior is happening. Don't wait for the end of your TV show. Delaying the time-out even five minutes only weakens your message and encourages your tot to push the limits even harder.

Use a Mirror. Put a mirror on the wall near your time-out area. That allows you to walk away, yet still observe your child (without him noticing you). Remember, during time-out you want your child to think you're totally ignoring him.

Don't Gloat or Shame Your Child. Saying, "You're bad! You need a time-out!" makes some tots feel worthless and others burn with resentment. It can spur your child to resist your limits even more the next time.

Q: Will my child get confused if I count "one, two, three" at other times, like play?
A: Nope. Remember, your message is carried in your tone of voice and gestures. Kids can easily tell the difference between playful counting and your serious face and voice, along with your finger raised in warning, signaling a time-out.

Q: Is time-out damaging? Can it hurt my child's psyche or break his spirit?
A: No. Respectfully putting a child into a short isolation is not traumatizing.

You've heard the expression "survival of the fittest"? Challenges make your toddler more resilient and emotionally fit. Your toddler is not a snowflake needing protection from all problems. He's a resilient and tenacious human being, and with your love and support he'll learn to bounce back from all of life's hardships.

But be careful of the words you use when you discipline your toddler. Young children *are* deeply hurt when we shame, embarrass, or demean them (see page 58).

Q: What should I do when my little boy fights being put into time-out?
A: Try to sidestep power struggles. Avoid comments like "You're so bad! Get in your room, immediately! Do you hear me?"

If your child resists time-out . . . calmly offer a choice. "I know you hate it, but you have to go. Do you want to walk or be carried?" If he won't, or can't, answer, carry your kicking, screaming cave-kid to the time-out place in as unemotional a manner as you can muster. You can be silent or repeat in Toddler-ese, "You *hate* it, you *hate* it!" as you carry him there.

Q: What should I do if my child has a tantrum while he is in time-out?
A: Spirited kids have spirited reactions . . . including *during* time-out. However, as long as the room is well childproofed, don't try to stop his yelling and throwing of things. If he sees that his actions *bug* you, it may actually make him get *wilder*.

Older tots who mess up the room during time-out need a warning that they'll have to stay in longer: "Phil, I know you're mad, but stop throwing or Mr. Dinger will give you a bigger time-out." When the time-out ends, he can come out, but after a few minutes, calmly require him to help you pick up his things before you resume playing with him.

Q: Can you do a time-out when you are not at home?
A: To prevent toddler misbehavior in public, plan short trips, describe what fun things you'll do while you're out, and feed the meter a lot during your errands. (It also helps to talk about the fun you will have once you return home.)

Sometimes, however, despite your best attempts, your child may need a time-out during your errands. If you're not far from the car, it's a handy time-out place. Here's what to do:

As always, start out by connecting with respect and offering a win-win compromise or distraction. If these fail, try a clap-growl, or proceed directly to counting to three, and if that doesn't stop the behavior go immediately to the car for the time-out.

Deposit him in the childproofed car (windows open a tiny bit, doors locked). Then stand right outside the car with your back turned to him. (Never walk away even for a second!)

After his time-out is up, take him out and use Toddler-ese to show you know how upset he was. Once he has calmed down, *do not* immediately return to your errands. First, give a small time-in to *grease the wheels* of cooperation. Then quickly finish your shopping or just go home.

Warning: Don't strap your child in the car seat during the time-out. You don't want him to associate this safety device with punishment. Also, never give your child a time-out in a hot car.

Should I Expect My Toddler to Say "I'm Sorry"?

All kids need to be taught manners. But apologizing after a misdeed may take a few years to learn. In general, quiet, shy kids learn to apologize faster than stubborn, challenging kids.

Try this: After your child misbehaves, ask for an apology, *but don't insist on one.* Making a huge issue about saying "sorry" only invites a power struggle. (Mom: "Say you're sorry!" Child: "No, you can't make me!" Mom: "I'm warning you!") You want to avoid battles you can't win . . . and *forcing* your tot to apologize is impossible if he really digs in his heels.

If your child shows no regret it's time for a little kind ignoring. Say, "You're still mad! You say, 'No way, I don't *want* to say I'm sorry!' Okay, sweetheart, I'll check on you in a minute and see how you're feeling."

Also, plant seeds of kindness by pointing out when other people apologize, and include apologies in your fairy tales and role-playing.

If your child *does* apologize, don't make a big deal out of it. Simply say "Thanks." But, later on, gossip to his toys or Grandma about how good you feel when he says he's sorry. And praise him during your bedtime sweet talk routine.

Q: What if he just plays while he's in time-out?

A: It doesn't matter. The purpose of time-out is not to make your child miserable, but to temporarily separate him from whatever he was doing, and from you.

Giving a Fine: A Penalty for Big Toddlers

Maura's twins, Jake and Pete, 36 months, were struggling over a red ball. Maura knew she needed to stop them before there was blood on the carpet! She tried a little impassioned FFR + Toddler-ese:

"Ball! Ball! Ball! You both want it! You want it now! You say mine!! My ball!" Then as they quieted for a second and looked at her, she said, "But noooo! No fighting, or Mommy takes ball away. Balls are for sharing." Then she offered a fun distraction, "Hey! I've got an idea! Let's all roll the ball together!"

Maura got them rolling it back and forth and then left them alone. Two minutes later, they were squabbling again. And again, she echoed their frustration. "Ball! Ball! You both want ball. But Mommy says, 'No fight . . . no fight!' So the ball has to go night-night. Say, 'Bye-bye, ball. See you later.' "

Despite their protests, Maura put the ball out of reach and said, "Come on, you rugrats! Let's have a race to the kitchen and we'll have a little snack. Do you want cheese or maybe some yummy mud?"

What It Is: If time-out is like going to jail, giving a fine is like, well, being fined. It's a "take-charge" consequence that targets your toddler's growing love of freedom and owner-ship.

Giving a fine penalizes your tot by removing a valued priv-ilege or toy. Make the punishment related to the misconduct. In other words, if he defies you by playing basketball in the house, remove the ball for a while. (Penalties that connect the punishment to the misbehavior are also called *logical* conse-quences.)

Best Used For: Toddlers two and up (especially three and up).

How It Works: Simple! If your child ignores your warning or repeatedly breaks an important rule, remove a privilege or possession that's directly linked to the misbehavior.

If your toddler conks a friend with his toy bat, take the bat away and end the playdate. Say, "No hit! No hit . . . no bat when you hit. Now we go home."

When you take away a privilege, tell your child you know how much she wants it, but what she's doing is not okay. For example, if your three-year-old refuses to stop tossing crack-ers to the dog, remove the crackers and say, "You like to see Rusty eat crackers, but crackers are for people . . . *not* dogs. Mommy said, 'Stop, no, no, no!' but Eleanor didn't listen to Mommy's words, so . . . bye-bye crackers. *No* crackers for dogs. Now you can get down and play."

In another example, if your two-year-old keeps dumping buckets of sand out of the sandbox after being warned to stop, remove him from the sandbox and say, "Mommy said, 'No dump sand! No dump sand!' It's a mess! So say, 'Bye-bye sand!' No more sandbox. Let's wash hands. . . . Do you want to dry your hands on one piece of paper or two?"

Sometimes the "prized possession" you remove is . . . you. This is using kind ignoring as a fine: "Mommy doesn't like it when you say those words. They don't make me laugh. They hurt my ears. I'm going to the kitchen and I'll be back in a little bit when you remember your nice words."

Once your toddler stops the negative behavior, do a little something that is fun to feed his meter and show him that good things happen when he follows the rules. Later, you might gossip to Daddy on the phone about when he did good listening and stopped when Mommy said stop.

If your child misbehaves in the same way every day, take a calm moment to discuss the fine you will be forced to give if he ignores your warning: "Honey, remember when you were playing with your ball in the house and Mommy said 'No!'? Well, the next time you bounce the ball in the house, Mommy has to take the ball away for a whole day."

Give your child extra chances to learn this lesson by role-playing with his dolls. (Have the Mommy doll tell the little boy doggie what you want him to do.)

Spanking: How *Not* to Punish a Toddler

When you're angry, clap . . . don't slap.

Violence is a huge problem in our country. And it has its roots in the home. After all, our toddlers imitate most things we do. If we eat with our fingers, they'll imitate. If we whistle while we work, they'll try to do that. So if we hit them when we don't like their actions, what do you think they learn from that?

Hitting children teaches them that it's okay for big people to hit little people and that it's okay to vent anger through violence. Is that really what you want your child to learn? And what sense does it make to spank kids to punish them for hitting? We don't teach children not to spit by spitting at them, do we?

Toddlers get spanked and slapped more than any other age group. Now, I know there will be times when your toddler will make you really mad. But when that happens, please *clap . . . don't slap.* Vent your anger by clapping and growling, not by shaking and slapping.

We expect our little toddler cave-kids to act primitive, but *we* can do better.

Spanking: Real-Life Questions

Q: If my son defies me when I say "No!," I give his hand a little swat. Is that okay?

A: Here's the problem with swatting—it's a dead-end street! What I mean is, as your child grows older, that "little swat" will no longer intimidate him. When he rebels, you'll be forced to hit him harder . . . and harder. Some parents eventually find themselves using belts, coat hangers, or sticks. And later, children get so big that even those things don't work.

Q: My father was spanked, and it made him behave, and he spanked me, and I behaved too. So what's the problem with me spanking my son?

A: I often hear parents say, "I was spanked, and I turned out okay." I'm a big supporter of family traditions. Many of them have great value, but spanking is not one we should be proud of. (God knows you would *never* allow anyone else to spank your child, would you?) Slapping can trigger feelings of resentment and humiliation that can fester for an entire lifetime (especially if we were unfairly punished, or hit out of anger, or in the face, or with an object).

I think the only reason spanking has been passed on—generation after generation—from the Dark Ages to today is because parents never knew there was a better alternative. In fact, I have *never* met a parent who said she would keep hitting her kids if she had another way to get them to behave that was easy, effective, and respectful.

Well, that's exactly what *The Happiest Toddler* approach offers. Simple methods help parents raise children who *want* to obey (out of love and respect), not children who are *forced* to obey (through threats and fear).

Your ancestors had many traditions that you have happily stopped. They washed clothes in streams, slept on hay mattresses, and used outhouses. In those "good ol' days," children were paddled, whipped with switches and belts, had their ears pulled . . . their faces slapped . . . their mouths washed out with soap . . . their tongues "hot-sauced" . . . and their knuckles rapped with rulers.

It's time to stop using intimidation and pain to make kids cooperate.

No offense, Grandpa, but there *is* a better way!

PART FOUR

How Do I Handle This One?

Now that you know the basics, let's put them to work in some all-too-typical toddler situations.

♦ **Chapter 8** zeroes in on the number one frustrating behavior that our toddlers level at us: temper tantrums. I give tantrums their own chapter because almost every toddler has them (and almost every parent asks me about them). Yet with these tips, you can actually shorten more than 50 percent of outbursts to just seconds, and prevent nine out of ten tantrums from occurring in the first place.

♦ **Chapter 9** reviews most of the rest of the challenging toddler behaviors that parents have to deal with at one time or another:

- ▪ worries and fears
- ▪ annoying attitudes and actions
- ▪ defiance
- ▪ aggressive and/or dangerous behavior

For all these tough situations, I'll discuss how you can use *The Happiest Toddler* tools to solve the problem and, in the process, raise a child who is confident, obedient, loving, and happy!

8

Taming
Tantrums . . . Like
Magic!

"*What makes me mad? Days when buttons
won't go straight and I want to stay up late and
I hate what's on my plate.*"
—Catherine and Laurence Anholt, *What Makes Me Happy*

Main Points:

- Tantrums are normal but avoidable.

- Tantrums peak between 18 and 24 months and again at around three and a half years of age.

- Tantrums "push our buttons" and make many of us overreact.

- To *stop* half of your toddler's tantrums in seconds: Connect with respect, and if that fails, add kind ignoring.

- To *prevent* 50 to 90 percent of outbursts from even happening: 1) avoid problem situations, 2) connect with respect . . . all day, 3) feed the meter, and 4) teach patience-stretching.

"Tess is bilingual—she talks and screams."

—Ted, dad of 20-month-old Tess

All toddlers have tantrums. . . . It's normal!

These little explosions can make us feel frustrated and attacked, but please don't take the wailing and flailing personally. Tantrums are not a sign that you're a bad parent or that you have a bad child. Even adults drop down an emotional elevator and act uncivilized when we're upset. But remember, our toddlers are pretty uncivilized to begin with, so when they get upset they often scratch, spit, shriek, and act *totally prehistoric*!

The good news is that the techniques in this chapter will help you to defuse most "screaming meanie" attacks as fast as a bomb squad.

But before looking at how to stop and prevent your toddler's meltdowns, I want to make sure you understand why almost all toddlers tantrum from time to time.

 ## Why Do Toddlers Have Tantrums?

Tantrums usually peak at 18 to 24 months, subside a little, and then peak again around three and a half years. At these ages your child's brain is virtually *bubbling over* with an intense and explosive mix of primitive impulses: greed, stubbornness, aggression, and impatience. And when you combine the "nitro" of your tot's passionate "Mine!" with the "glycerine" of your adamant "No way!" . . . you've got some really, really powerful TNT. *Kapow!*

Other factors that push our sweet little toddlers into maniac mode include:

They Don't Speak Well. Wouldn't you get frustrated if you lived somewhere you couldn't speak the language? Well, your toddler also gets irritated when she can't communicate. No wonder little kids with limited language skills often resort to nontalking forms of communication like foot stomping, arm waving, eye bulging, and screaming!

We Set a Bad Example. Venting your anger in front of your child may train her to scream more. She'll learn that unleashing her rage is totally fine. *After all . . . Mommy does it.*

They Get Stuck in an Emotional Corner. For many little Tarzans, forcing them to give in can make them feel *humiliated.* When their primitive sense of pride gets bruised, they go bonkers. The harder these kids struggle against us, the more they get painted into an emotional "corner," unable to gracefully back down and recover from their upset.

> *Jeev, 18 months, was a gentle boy, but he could still act pretty uncivilized. He loved eating whole pears . . . but one day his mom, Suparna, cut his pear in pieces because it was extra juicy. His response? He grabbed the plate and hurled it at his mom's head! Suparna realized her "mistake" and immediately offered Jeev a whole pear. And what did this little cave-kid do? He scowled, shook his head No! and refused to even look at it.*

Like Jeev, your toddler may get so upset she paints herself into a corner, unable to give in, even when you offer *exactly what she's asking for.* That's why respectful, diplomatic skills are so great. They help our tots escape from this predicament with their pride intact.

They Have "Temper" Temperaments. Intense and spirited toddlers have bigger meltdowns because, well, they do *everything* bigger. You can't change your child's temperament, but the tips in this book will help you keep him from exploding into anger with every frustration and disappointment.

Our World Is Simultaneously Too Exciting . . . and Too Boring. Your toddler's immature brain may get overloaded by noisy DVDs and fast-paced TV. Yet at the same time, she may get bored spending a lot of time at home. Remember, up until 200 years ago, toddlers usually spent many, many hours a day playing outdoors.

Tantrums Work! When we give in to outbursts (or pay too much attention to them), our kids learn that screaming gets them what they want. Younger toddlers recognize this subconsciously, but older ones often learn to intentionally use fits to get their way.

Today's parents face many tough challenges. On top of working full-time jobs outside the home (which over half of all moms with kids under the age of three do), they cook and clean and do housekeeping chores, and they may be responsible for the care and feeding of their parents and/or grandparents, too. These days, most parents shoulder these responsibilities without much assistance from neighbors, kin, babysitters, or other hired help.

Whew! No wonder it feels like you're giving 120 percent . . . you are.

You try *so* hard. You do *so* much. That's why it can really push your buttons when your toddler turns into a screaming red-eyed bully. It can feel so unfair—even humiliating—especially if she pelts you with mean words, like "I hate you!" or "You're stupid!"

Our toddler's rage can suddenly push us over the edge into our own impulsive, irrational rage.

We've all been there, but when it happens we must try to remember to breathe and say to ourselves: *My child* is the caveman. . . . *I'm* a civilized adult.

And as a civilized adult, you must try to stay calm and not return your child's outbursts with sarcasm, humiliation, or removal of your love . . . and certainly not with violence. (Review Chapter 2 for more ideas on how to handle your strong feelings.)

Why Does My *Three-Year-Old* Still Have Tantrums?

As kids get older and more verbal, their tantrums occur less and less. Yet many three-to-four-year-olds (and teens) have occasional meltdowns. That's because:

1. **They *still* struggle with impulse control.** *Older toddlers are increasingly well behaved. But after a long day, your child may lose control and scream with the force of Old Faithful (especially if he has a spirited temperament).*
2. **They are emotional yo-yos.** *Three-year-olds are no longer babies, but they're not quite big kids. They sometimes yo-yo back and forth between these two developmental stages so much that they totally fall apart: "I'm a baby! . . . I'm a big kid!" Yikes! Think of it as emotional whiplash (for him and you).*
3. **They see outbursts at home.** *If there is lots of quarreling in your family (or violence displayed on TV), your child may defy you more because he's learned that arguing is a normal way to express frustration.*

Here is an effective way to lovingly halt most toddler tantrums . . . in under a minute. By now, these tantrum-calming skills should sound quite familiar. They're as close to a magic wand as you'll ever get.

Stop a Tantrum by Connecting with Respect

When your toddler starts to *lose it,* the first thing you should do is connect with respect. Squat down to his level and echo back a bit of his feelings by using the Fast-Food Rule and Toddler-ese. (Remember to use your tone of voice and gestures to reach your child's sweet spot.) Practice this several times on small eruptions before trying it out on a major outburst. Amazingly, at least 50 percent of the time this simple step alone will quell tantrums in seconds.

> *"Mad . . . mad . . . mad! Sara mad! Sara wants
> cookie . . . now! Cookie!!"*

Parents who respond by immediately voicing their adult views or distraction are like impatient fast-food order-takers who jump right to *their* message ("You owe five dollars") without repeating the order. That's why answering your two-year-old's whines for a premeal cookie by narrating her feelings ("Cookie! *Cookie! You* want cookie! You want cookie, *now!*") provokes *less* crying than jumping right to your message, "No, honey. No cookies before dinner!"

Once your child begins to quiet, it becomes *your* turn to give a message ("But nooo, sweetheart. You know the rule: Cookies are *after* dinner.").

> Linda used this approach to neatly sidestep a potentially unsafe struggle when her toddler loudly protested getting out of the bathtub:

> "Our three-year-old, Jasmine, hates getting out of the tub. She would stay in there all day if she could. One day, when it was time for her to get out I gave her the two-minute warning and the one-minute warning. Then I turned the water off and she freaked and started yelling, 'No! No! I don't want to get out; I don't want to get out.'

> "I remembered the Toddler-ese and I energetically waved my finger, frowned a bit, and echoed her words, 'No, no, *no! I don't* want to get out! I want to stay in the bathtub! *I don't* want to get out!'

> "I was stunned! Within seconds, she just looked at me and stopped crying.

> "Then, in a calmer voice I said, 'Jasmine, I know you don't want to get out, but it's time to go; we have to get ready to see Daddy.' And she stood up and got out. Then I dried her fast and played dolls with her for a few minutes to thank her for her cooperation. It was great."

After you give your message, you can encourage your child to be even more cooperative in the future if you take a moment to feed her meter with a little distraction or a win-win compromise:

- **Distraction:** Once your child starts to calm, offer a bit of fun (like attention, a hug, a snack, or playing the boob). Playing the boob, for example, shows your tot that even though she had to give in to you *this time*, there are plenty of other times when she gets to be faster/smarter/stronger than you.

    Point at her shoe and beg her, in a pitiful voice, to give it to you. When she hesitates, throw your hands down like you "give up" and say, "Okay, you win, you always win me."

> A few seconds later, beg for her shoe again
> and let her reject you again. Kids love when
> we're boobs and they get to reject our silly
> requests.

- **Offer a win-win compromise:** Right after you squelch a tantrum, help your child save face by offering her some type of compromise. This little deal shows your toddler that even though she lost the argument you have respect for her and she can still hold her head up high.

> "Cracker . . . cracker . . . You want cracker!
> You want cracker . . . right now! No crackers
> now, honey, but after your carrots you can
> have more crackers. Should you get two or
> three?"

But . . . what if all your good communication is met with even louder bawling? Then it's time to offer a hug, solve the problem, or do a little kind ignoring:

- **Offer a hug.** Your toddler may just be having a bad day . . . we've all been there. Try offering your upset child a hug, but be prepared to duck (just in case your irate little Tarzan takes a swing at your nose). Some parents soothe their flailing furious toddlers by giving a bear hug from behind—restraining the arms—while they repeatedly whisper in the ear things like "You're really, really mad." "You say, 'No, no, *no!*' "
- **Solve the problem.** Occasionally, if you're really in a time crunch, it's okay to give in. For example, you

might say to your upset three-year-old, "You're so sad! You really want a cookie . . . now! The rule is no cookies before dinner . . . but you were so helpful picking up your toys this morning, Mommy will bend the rule—a tiny bit—and give you one cookie. Do you want it in a napkin or on a plate?"

- **Kind ignore.** If your uncivilized little friend is still flailing on the floor, most of the time your best tactic will be to lovingly give her the *cold shoulder*—kind ignoring (see page 180). Here's how:
- **Use Toddler-ese** one last time . . . then lovingly say you're leaving for a little while.

Be caring, but matter-of-fact. Avoid threats, sarcasm, or shaming. Kind ignoring makes it clear that you understand, but you're not giving in.

- Pretend to be busy doing something for twenty seconds.
- If your child starts to calm, quickly turn to your tot and offer some Toddler-ese, a hug, and a nice time-in ("You were really sad. . . . You wanted the ball and Mommy said 'No!' But come on . . . let's play with your trains. Do you want to be Thomas or Henry?").
- If your child is still crying after twenty seconds of being ignored, return and echo again how she's feeling. Many kids get so upset that they need us to do kind ignoring two to three times before they start to settle.

A few spirited kids just won't stop crying even after you come and go a few times. They have trouble giving in because it hurts their pride. If your child is one of these stub-

born kids, you may need to ignore him for two to five minutes until he starts to calm. Keep a watch on him out of the corner of your eye or in a mirror. Once he stops crying and starts to play with something, just sit on the ground near him (to show respect). Don't be in a rush to talk or make eye contact; remember, he's probably still mad. Then, start to reconnect by slowly joining in his activity. Don't talk about the tantrum yet. Just reward the now-good behavior with a bit of your attention. That will help him get over his pouting and open his heart again.

Public Meltdowns: How Not to Panic in the Streets

Public tantrums are especially tough because, well, they're so *public.* They make us feel like we're under a magnifying glass and everyone is *staring at our flaws.* What's more, many toddlers turn up the shrieking if we seem embarrassed or unsure how to respond.

Avoiding *aisle-three meltdowns* is a lot easier if you plan ahead. Keep your trips short, organized, and timed to when your child will not be tired or hungry. (Meandering aimlessly through a mall is sensory overload for a little Stone Age brain.) Also, make waits easier by bringing along little snacks or treats (like stickers, drawing materials, or "tagalong" toys that your child gets only when you are out on errands). If, however, these best of intentions don't work out as planned, you can stop tantrums fast . . . the *Happiest Toddler* way. Here's a great example of how one mother used connecting with respect to short-circuit her child's tantrum.

Sandy brought Corey, 22 months, to the toy store while his sister, Chrissy, shopped for a present. It was their third stop that morning. Sandy sat Corey before a display of toy trains, keeping a close watch while she helped Chrissy.

When it was time to go, Corey refused. Sandy made a weak stab at using the FFR. "I know you don't want to go, sugar, but we're late and I don't have time for this right now."

Then Sandy went to pick Corey up and he erupted in tears. The clerk frowned, Chrissy moaned, and Sandy checked her watch. Corey should have had lunch and a nap an hour earlier.

Ignoring the stares of the other shoppers, Sandy realized she needed to do a better job of connecting with respect. Kneeling next to him, she exclaimed, "You say, 'No! No, no, nooooo!' You say, 'No go home! No! Corey likes trains!' Corey says, 'No go home!' "

Corey's crying weakened a bit and he stopped flailing, so Sandy continued. She stomped her foot, shook her head, and waved her arms to

echo some of her son's intensity. "You say, 'No!
No, no, no! Nooooo!' You say, 'NO go home! Corey
not ready!' " Magically, Corey stopped crying.

> *Then Sandy dropped her voice to a whisper.*
"Hey! Psssst! Hey! Let's play train. We'll be the
train. . . . Choo-choo! Choo-choo! Let's choo-choo
all the way to the car."

> *Chrissy was so embarrassed that she*
pretended she didn't know her chug-a-chugging
mother and brother, but Corey was thrilled to
make train noises and held on to his mom's hips
all the way out the door.

See the section on tantrum triggers (page 225) for more tips on tantrum prevention.

A Scary Tantrum Side Effect: Breath-Holding

Q: My toddler screamed so hard he passed out! I was terrified. How can I keep that from ever happening again?

A: Breath-holding during a tantrum looks really scary, but fortunately it's usually not a big deal. Typically what happens is that young toddlers (15- to 30-month-olds) suddenly get upset (mad, scared, or startled) and try to cry, but although their mouths open, no sound comes out. For thirty to forty seconds, they keep getting bluer (or paler) until they pass out. (Sometimes the body may twitch a little too.)

In essence, these kids "forget" to breathe! But the instant they pass out, their breathing starts again automatically, and they revive in seconds.

If you can reach your child *before* he passes out, wet your hand and sprinkle a little cool water right in his face or puff hard a few inches from his face for several seconds (like you're blowing out birthday candles). This can often prevent a spell and make the child gasp, sputter, and start breathing.

Simple breath-holding spells are not dangerous. There is no risk of injury (as long as they don't fall and hit their heads). Nevertheless, you should immediately call your doctor to make sure it wasn't due to a seizure or other medical condition (like anemia). Ask if your child needs an iron supplement to keep the spells from happening again.

How to Eliminate Most Tantrums . . . Before They Even Start!

Being able to calm tantrums in seconds will make you feel great, but you'll feel like the best, smartest, and happiest parent ever when you can stop the tantrums *before* they happen!

Now you're ready to join the thousands of parents who have eliminated 50 to 90 percent of their young child's tantrums *in less than a week.* The four key steps are:

1. Avoid problem situations.

2. Connect with respect . . . all day long.

3. Feed the meter.

4. Teach patience-stretching and magic breathing.

Step 1: Avoid Problem Situations

Nobody knows your toddler better than you. So I bet you already have a pretty good idea of which situations knock him off balance. The trick is to think ahead and be prepared.

The most common avoidable tantrum triggers are:

- **Fatigue.** Many kids get ornery if they miss their nap or sleep poorly at night.
- **Hunger.** Some kids get fussy if their meal is even thirty minutes late (low blood sugar). The moms of these sensitive tykes need to carry emergency snacks, like crackers and cheese, in the diaper bag.
- **Caffeine and stimulants.** Many kids bounce off the walls after having caffeinated drinks (cola, iced tea, chocolate milk). In addition, too much sugar or decongestants in cold medicines can also be *monster-makers*.
- **Being cooped up.** Toddlers thrive on outdoor play. Little cave-kids who don't get to *roam the jungle* (your backyard or the park) two or three times a day often get unbearably grumpy.
- **Being ignored.** Toddlers often act up when we ignore them for too long. That is why feeding the meter by playing the boob and giving time-ins—several times an hour—can miraculously reduce your child's need for time-outs.
- **Being overtempted.** If you live in a house with lots of attractive breakables, your little one may just not have enough self-control to keep his hands off things.
- **Unexpected changes.** Shy or sensitive kids may go bonkers when they have to deal with unexpected

changes. You can sidestep problems with these little "princess and the pea" people by reviewing your next day's plan, mentioning any changes in routine that might occur.

■ **Tension and violence.** Keep the peace in your house. Many toddlers model the violence they see on TV or when their parents fight at home.

Step 2: Connect with Respect . . . All Day Long

Don't just use your good communication skills to handle emotional explosions. Try to use the FFR and Toddler-ese dozens of times a day. Use them even when you're just dealing with a minor upset or a small request. For example, when your 18-month-old asks for juice, smile and narrate back his desire in a cheery voice, "You say, juicey! You love your juicey, mmm! Okay, sweetheart, *here's* your juice."

Help your child learn by your example as you use the FFR with others (other children, your partner . . . even your child's stuffed animals!). And comment to him about the feelings of people you see in magazines or in public. ("Honey, look how that man is whistling and happy! What do you think he is so happy about?")

Sure, all this takes a few extra seconds, but it pays off in ways big and small. Besides, your good communication will help your toddler learn how to talk and teach that loving people speak to each other with respect.

Step 3: Feed the Meter

Little 18-month-olds take—and take—and then they pressure us for more! They have short memories and forget the caring attention and fun play you just shared two hours before. (Remember, two hours feels like six to an impatient toddler.) But they need frequent bits of our loving attention as much as flowers need water and sunshine. That's why feeding the meter with green-light techniques—several times an hour—is such a powerful tool for preventing tantrums.

Parents who feed the meter many times a day make their kids feel smart, strong, respected, and loved. And, when kids feel like winners, they instantly become more cooperative.

Use: time-ins (like attention, play, praise, gossip, hand checks, stickers, hand stamps), confidence builders (like respectful listening, offering options, playing the boob), fun routines (like special time and bedtime sweet talk), and planting seeds of kindness (like fairy tales, catching others being good, and role-play).

Can small steps like playing catch, being a boob, and little nightly massages really head off conflicts? *Yes!* Your toddler understands that the more play and attention you give him—and the more you build his confidence—the more cooperation he owes *you*.

But remember this key point: Your child's idea of what's *fair* is when he wins 90 percent of the time (see page 167). So if you let him feel smart and cared about oodles of times a day and let him get his way on many little "conflicts" you don't really care about (like what socks to wear or what book to read first), he'll give in much more (like eating a bite of vegetables or holding hands when you cross the street).

Step 4: Teach Patience

This fourth step, teaching patience, is critically important to preventing tantrums. Patience-stretching and magic breathing help our little cave-kids strengthen their brains' ability to control their primitive impulses. Children who learn to be patient just a little bit longer automatically become calmer and more reasonable. And that extra minute or two of your tot's patient waiting is often just enough for you to finish the chore you're working on (get off the phone, finish tossing the salad, etc.).

Please review the instructions for teaching patience-stretching and magic breathing (pages 122 and 125). Practice patience-stretching *several times a day* (with older tots also do magic breathing once or twice a day). Within a week, you'll be thrilled with your child's growing ability to handle frustrations and delay his need for instant gratification.

Each time your little friend patiently waits for something, reward his cooperation with a tiny time-in or some playing the boob so he knows his efforts are appreciated.

Aneta and Tony were struggling on a daily basis with their three young boys. Oliver, the oldest, was a great guy, but he had always been a strong-willed handful. So when the twins, Lucas and Mattheo, entered toddlerhood, Aneta started to feel "triple-teamed."

Aneta came to my office asking for help with discipline, especially to get control of two-year-old Lucas, who was driving them crazy with his screams, demands, and defiance. I taught her the Fast-Food Rule and Toddler-ese and the *Happiest Toddler* tricks for stopping tantrums, and we put together a plan to start feeding the twins little one-minute bits of fun (attention, play, gossip, playing the boob, etc.) a couple of times an hour and one five-minute special time a day for each of the boys. And as she left, I asked Aneta to keep track of the number and intensity of the outbursts for the next week.

Aneta immediately started feeding the meter by paying attention to the boys when they were good and using kind ignoring and time-outs to handle the meltdowns. She and Tony particularly liked gossip, patience-stretching, and special time, and after a couple of days they started to feel more comfortable with Toddler-ese and playing the boob.

*I was supposed to call Aneta at the end of the
week to check on her progress, but she beat me
to the punch and called me one day early . . .
almost giggling with a feeling of success! She said
that initially Lucas's tantrums escalated for two
days, but then the kind ignoring worked like a
charm to reduce his eruptions from several
minutes to just seconds. But even better, all the
kids were being more patient and about 75
percent of all the tantrums had just disappeared!
She proudly exclaimed, "They're happier kids
and we're a happier family!"*

You can be sure that many people will give you many tips on
handling temper tantrums. Of course, you'll need to be strict
with your children from time to time, but as you practice the
advice in this chapter you'll soon see that the best way to convert a wild child into a happy tot is not with threats and force,
but with respect, encouragement, consistency, and play.

The time you spend with your children is the best, smartest
investment you will ever make. All the generosity you give now
will be repaid to you and your family and community one
hundred times in the future. As your child grows up, you'll
avoid countless arguments, lies, struggles, and dangerous displays just because you made this investment of time and effort
to learn how to give your child a loving, happy start to life.

Now that you're getting tantrums under control, you're
ready to learn how to combine all the techniques you mastered in the previous chapters to help you expertly handle almost any other situation your toddler throws your way.

9

Real Answers to Common Problems

"*In the middle of every difficulty lies opportunity.*"

—Albert Einstein

Main Points:

Troublesome toddler behaviors usually fall into one of four categories:

- worries and fears
- annoying attitudes and actions
- defiance
- aggressive and/or dangerous behavior

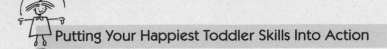

Tears, fears, and the occasional tug-of-war are all par for the course when living with toddlers. But that doesn't mean you're powerless to make things better. On the contrary, this last chapter will help you use the whole doctor's bag of *Happiest Toddler* tools and skills to solve almost any challenge your young child will throw at you. (Note: For a quick review, read a description of each *Happiest Toddler* skill in the "Key Terms and All-Star Tricks" section on page 285.)

Most of the problem behaviors parents have to deal with during these years fall into one of four main groups:

1. **Worries and fears.** *Examples:* separation worries, fears, abandonment issues when a new baby arrives.

2. **Annoying attitudes and actions.** *Examples:* dawdling, interrupting, whining.

3. **Defiance.** *Examples:* refusing medicine, fighting the car seat, picky eating.

4. **Aggressive and/or dangerous behavior.** *Examples:* attacks on other children (hitting, pinching, biting), running away.

 Behavior Challenge #1: Worries and Fears

Some tykes meet new people and situations with bouncy confidence. They jump right in and away they go. But for other little kids, worries lurk around every corner. These easily rattled children often:

- have a shy, slow-to-warm-up temperament
- are stressed (hungry, tired, bored, sick, facing big challenges, etc.)
- had a really scary experience in the past

What can you do to help these kids overcome their fears? In a word: lots! Let's look at a few examples. . . .

Worried-Behavior Example: Separation Worries

When your little one begs you not to *abandon* her at pre-school (or at the babysitter's or at bedtime), it can be tough to handle. Sad eyes and clingy pleas really pull at the heartstrings!

Here's how Mari uses the Fast-Food Rule and Toddler-ese to handle her son's separation worries:

> *"When my two-year-old, Aidan, arrives at school he usually shrieks, 'I want Mama!' and he won't exit the car. So I help him by narrating his feelings with a bit of intensity to hit his sweet spot: 'No, Mama! No, no, no! No school! No teacher Chris! No teacher Cindy! No friends! I want Mama! No school!'*
>
> *"By then, he usually starts calming, and I offer a compromise: 'Okay, okay. No problem! But we have to tell teacher Chris that Aidan says, "No school today." So let's go. You carry teddy for me, okay?'*
>
> *"At this point Aidan always leaves the car with me. Once inside school, we stop and play a little or chat with the teacher. Most days, he quickly gets involved in the buzz of activity and*

*his friends and kisses me good-bye in just five or
ten minutes!"*

Mari's words make Aidan feel accepted and safe. The little compromise she offers shows her respect and helps persuade him to exit the car and enter the school without a fight.

Luckily, Mari has the time to either wait with Aidan or take him home if he continues crying. But many other parents don't have that luxury; they *must* leave their child in order to go to work. If that's your situation, use a combination of some of the tools that have been described in earlier chapters and practice them first at home, so they'll work better in a stressful situation.

Tools to Handle Separation Worries

Patience-Stretching. Practice the following three techniques for several days to help prepare your child for easier separations. Start with a few seconds and gradually increase to a minute. She'll quickly learn that waiting is cool because when she's patient she usually gets what she wants (see page 122).

Fairy Tales. Prepare your child for what is to come by telling little stories in which Mommy goes away . . . but always comes back.

> *"Once upon a time there was a little birdie
> named Fluffy who worried when her mommy
> flew away to find breakfast. She said, 'Don't go,
> Mommy!' But her mommy had to leave . . . for
> just a super-duper fast minute. So Fluffy waited
> and sang songs with her teddy bear until*

Mommy came back. Mommy *always* came back,
and then Fluffy felt happy and safe. 'Yea!
Mommy's home!' the little birdie cheered, and
her mom gave her lots of kisses . . . and some big
juicy worms to eat."

Loveys. Loveys are terrific for kids with separation issues. Encourage your tot to *make friends* with a lovey. If your older toddler hasn't yet taken to one, offer a special *charm* (like a bracelet, magic coin, photo) that she can touch and look at whenever she misses you.

Now, after practicing these at home for several days, here's how to use them to respond to your child's protests at preschool. I call this combination of tools "Mommy Interruptus."

Start by Connecting with Respect. Give hugs and echo your child's concerns in a sincere voice with lots of repetition: "You say, 'No! No, *No!!! No* school! *No* go, Mommy!' "

Once your tot calms a bit, give her a little time-in (play, read, or sit together as you describe what other kids are wearing and doing).

Next, Use Patience-Stretching and Loveys. After a few minutes, act like you suddenly remembered you have to do something: "Oh! Oh! Wait! *Wait!* Mommy has to see teacher. Wait! Wait!" Then say, "You hold teddy (or your magic bracelet) really hard, and Mommy will be right back!" Then walk quickly across the room and return in just two or three seconds, saying, "I know, sweetheart. You say, 'Mommy, don't go!' But, good waiting! *Good waiting!* Come on, let's play!"

If she's protests, reflect her feelings by hitting her sweet spot with your face, tone, and gestures. Play a little more, until she is happy for a few minutes; then repeat the patience-

stretching. For example, you might suddenly say, "Uh-oh! Pee-pee! Pee-pee! Mommy has to go pee-pee. Here, hug teddy, I'll be right back." Then leave the room for a quick three seconds.

Over the next fifteen minutes, repeat this process many times. ("Uh-oh! Mommy has to pee-pee again! Here, let me draw a funny face on your hand you can look at, and I'll be right back.") Gradually leave for longer periods (ten seconds, twenty seconds, thirty seconds, one minute).

Once your child can calmly handle several minutes without you, you can leave for good. But never sneak away! Give a big wave and cheerfully announce, "Bye-bye! I love you. I'll see you after your nap. If you want me, just touch your *magic* bracelet (or look at the funny face I drew on your hand) and think of me giving you a big hug." You might also mention something fun you'll do together after school.

Finally, the *Icing on the Cake:* Praise + Gossip. When you pick her up at the end of the day, praise your tot's success (give her a star or hand check). At home, gossip to Grandma or Daddy about her courage: "Darcy told me, 'No, no. Don't go. . . ,' but then she saw fun toys and some fun big girls and she was brave. She had a silly time and ate snack . . . a big cracker with juice! Then Mommy came back, and gave Darcy a *big* hug and we were happy!"

Note: Some strong-willed kids cry when you leave, despite all your preparation. If that happens with your tot, call the school twenty minutes after you leave her, and ask the teacher if she is still crying. If she reports, "She started playing happily two minutes after you left," take a deep breath and congratulate yourself. (Fortunately, this is what happens nine times out of ten.)

However, if your child won't stop crying after you leave, something else may be fueling her anxiety. If there are stresses at home (like a new baby, divorce, etc.), plan to stay at school all day, for a few days, to monitor the situation. If you can't stay, try to pay some surprise visits to make sure the kids and teachers are treating her well. Keep using playing the boob, fairy tales, role-playing, patience-stretching, magic breathing, etc., to boost her self-confidence at home.

If the fussing continues, consider changing schools or sitters.

Worried-Behavior Example: Sudden New Fears

Fear is a common problem for toddlers and often comes on without warning. Typical fears include monsters, snakes, spiders, attackers, the dark, and being abandoned, but your tot could develop a fear of almost anything—including clowns! (As a young child I was afraid of a closet in our laundry room where my parents kept a recording of *Sleeping Beauty*. . . . It had a scary witch's voice on it.)

> *Stella, three, was smart and confident. So the day she spied an ant crawling up her leg, her*

hysterical crying came from out of the blue. Her mom, Fran, removed the tiny bug, reassured her daughter, and then they both promptly forgot the whole incident . . . or so it seemed.

The next day, however, Stella complained that she was afraid to sit in the grass because of the "buggies." Fran persuaded her to play outside by tucking her pants into her socks to "protect her." But that night things got worse. Once in bed, Stella cried out: "Go! Go! Mommy! M-O-M-M-Y!!!" Fran arrived seconds later and little Stella clung to her for dear life, sobbing, "Buggies, Mommy! BUGGIES!"

Fran turned on the lights to show Stella her bed was bug-free. "See, honey? No bugs! Everything's okay. See? No buggies!" Stella slowly calmed and Fran left. But a minute later Stella burst into a panicked cry about "buggies" yet again. That night Stella slept in her parents' bed, where she was calm and quiet the whole night.

Fears may pop up when a child is under stress, suffers a scary experience (an injury, earthquake, car accident), sees a scary cartoon, or hears something ordinary but misinterprets it as something frightening. ("At the picnic, the ants carried away *everything*!")

Young toddlers (especially shy, cautious kids) often fear loud sounds like thunder, firecrackers, or barking dogs. Around age three, fear of "bad men," monsters, and witches often develop.

One reason fears pop up at this age is because of a three-year-old's new ability: *comparing*. Three-year-olds constantly compare themselves to the rest of the world. And, as you might imagine, the world can look pretty big and scary to them. Toddlers love puffing out their chests and announcing their supremacy over babies, but they often feel weak and vulnerable compared to big kids, big dogs, and big strangers.

Older toddlers also have fears because of something called *projection*. Many bigger tots still have the urge to bite and hit, but they know that their parents expect them to control these primitive impulses. So they transfer the urge from themselves and *project* it onto scary shadows, strangers, and assorted imaginary "meanies." ("The monster took my toys . . . and tried to pinch me!")

Note: Your reaction to your toddler's fears may be deeply rooted in your past. If *your* childhood fears were pooh-poohed, you may tend to overprotect your frightened child and accidentally undermine her confidence. On the other hand, if your family made a big deal out of praising you for courage, you may see your tot's fearfulness as a weakness that must be nipped in the bud.

I invite you to try to find a middle ground. Listen to your child's fear without minimizing it or overreacting. During three decades of pediatrics, I've noticed that frightened kids calm fastest when their worries are respectfully acknowledged and when they're encouraged to take baby steps to confront their fears.

Tools to Relieve Fears

First, show your child that you take her feelings seriously.

Connect with Respect. Toddler fears may start out small, but ignoring her fears will only make them grow. *We* know that ants aren't a danger, but if you're too fast to pooh-pooh your child's fear it may make her feel more alone . . . and *more* scared, just when she needs your help. So before you try to dispel her worries, invest a minute of your time in using the Fast-Food Rule and Toddler-ese to show your little friend that you "get it" and you really care.

> *"Bugs! Bugs! Stella hates buggies! Stella hates buggies! She says, 'Go away now, you buggies!'"*

Routines. Bedtime fears are made better by some loveys (cuddly protectors that "stand in" for you when you're in the next room) and special bedtime routines. Put on soothing music and dim the lights in your house an hour before bedtime to help keep your child in a calm state of mind. (Avoid roughhousing and TV during that *golden hour*.)

> *Fran gave Stella a bedtime massage (right after she did her magic breathing). Then Fran tucked her into bed and did a little bedtime sweet talk (listing great things she did that day and her fun plans for tomorrow). Then Fran kissed all Stella's dollies good-night and ended the routine with a few squirts of "secret superspray" (water with a tiny bit of lavender oil in a small spray bottle with a smiley-face sticker) and a special song ("Mommy loves you, Daddy loves you, Stella. Stella is safe, safe, safe!").*
>
> *The first night, Stella was fine for five minutes, but then she came crying to her parents' door. They listened and echoed her concerns (making sure they aimed for her sweet spot). Then Fran hugged her, walked her back to her room, and tucked her back into bed. Fran kissed the dollies good-night, sprayed the "secret superspray," sang the special song again . . . and went out. And that was it for the night. The next night Stella slept beautifully.*

*Within five nights, Fran was able to start
cutting back to her old, briefer bedtime routine.
And you know what? A few weeks later, for
Halloween, Stella begged Fran to go trick-or-
treating dressed up as an ant!*

Gossip. Let your child overhear you talking to her dollies about her fear. And use gossip to reward your tyke's little acts of bravery; for example, petting a neighbor's puppy or climbing up the slide. Each time she takes another baby step forward, gossip to her toys about her courage.

Win-Win Compromise. For toddlers, every day is filled with amazing, incredible sights! That's why they strongly believe that almost *anything's* possible. (Ghosts? Sure. Monsters? Of course! Your boss "exploded" at you today? Okay, but it sounds messy!) Using logic to deny a panicked child's fears ("There *are* no monsters!") is as doomed to failure as telling someone who fears flying that planes are safer than cars. The fear is very real in the imagination.

Here's a better approach: Wait for the panic to subside a bit, then offer a win-win compromise that allows your tot to feel safe and enables you to calm her hysteria. For example, you might suggest: temporarily letting her sleep with you; allowing your dog to keep her company; getting a Mickey Mouse night-light, etc.

Fairy Tales and Role-Play. Use the "side door" of your child's mind to help lessen her fears. Have her dollies "talk to each other" about the things that scare them . . . and how they calm themselves. Tell stories about nice doggies that lick your fingers and never bite and about mean doggies who have to go to time-out when they do something bad; role-play about dogs and encourage her to remind the puppy to be nice and not to bite.

> *To help her three-year-old, Myles, get over his*
> *fear of dogs, Maria would play "Puppy Pretend"*
> *with her little guy: "Honey, do you want to be*
> *the big dog with sharp teeth and scare me? Or do*
> *you want me to be the dog and you can be*
> *brave?" And at night she would put his cuddly*
> *dog doll right next to him in bed to keep the bad*
> *dogs away.*

Magic Breathing. Calm breathing helps children learn how to keep panic under control. If you have an older toddler, I recommend you practice it every day . . . *especially* if she is anxious or fearful.

For example, if your child is upset about a dog, first connect with respect ("You say, 'No, *no*, doggie . . . no!' Say, 'You go *away*, doggie! Go *away*!' Wow, that doggie was a little scary, huh?"). Then, once she calms, do some magic breathing. This will help her complete her calming and feel some mastery over the fear.

Confidence Builders. Making your child feel big and strong can also help her overcome fears. Practice boosting her overall confidence (listen with respect, ask her opinion, play the boob) once or twice an hour. And take some specific steps to build her confidence about the thing she fears. For example, if she's petrified by bugs, read books about bugs, cut bug pictures out of magazines to make a scrapbook, etc.

> *Fran found a library book to read to Stella*
> *showing that bugs lived in the dirt (not in kids'*

beds) and that they ate leaves ("They think kids taste yucky! Phooey!"). The pictures showed how tiny a bug is and how big a kid is. And Stella loved for her mom to draw a picture of a bug on a piece of paper and then she would crumple it up and throw it in the trash as she demanded, "Bad bug! Go away! Don't scare Stella!"

Using a bit of magic is another fun, confidence-building approach that really makes sense to a toddler's immature brain. Here's how some skillful parents *magically* soothed their toddlers' fears:

"Molly says, 'Go away, monsters! I don't like you!' But, honey, did you know that mommy monsters don't let their little boy and girl monsters go out at night? Yup. They have to eat their dinners and go right to bed! But to be 'double-triple' sure, let's do some secret magic to make 100 percent sure those monsters stay far, far away. 'Abracadabra, alakazaam, monsters, go home. . . . Don't come where I am!' " [Remember, "secret" and "magic" are two little words that make toddlers feel powerful.]

"Charlie, do you know what I just remembered? Dinosaurs hate the smell of garlic. They say, 'Yucky . . . poop!' Oh! And you know what? We are so lucky, because I saved the very best piece of superstrong garlic in the refrigerator. Yea! Let's rub a tiny bit on a piece of paper and put it by the window. That will keep them away for sure!"

Tess, three, became terrified when the smoke
alarm accidentally went off. To help her start
regaining her confidence, her parents named it
Fred and they taped a smiley face to it that Tess
had drawn. Twice a day they all went to the
alarm to say, "Good morning, Fred!" and "Good
night, Fred!" and when Tess was eating her snack
they said to Fred, "No way, Fred! No cookies for
you. Cookies are for kids!" Within a few days,
Tess's worry had become just a distant memory.

More Magic Fear-Fighters

Older toddlers love magic and pretend too. Try the following and see how fast the bad things go away:

- Offer a protective charm: a special "magic bracelet," a
  dreamcatcher (for bad dreams), a bedside photo of his
  protectors (like Mom and Dad or Superman), or, like
  Fran, a spray bottle of superspecial "magic water."
- Pretend to put an invisible "magic space suit" on your
  little one each night. Patiently massage it on from head
  to toe so it will keep him safe once he's in bed. Draw a
  picture of what he would look like in it . . . if he could
  see it.

Worried-Behavior Example: Struggles When a New Baby Arrives

Big changes are tough even on adults, so it's to be expected
that they give toddlers extra stress.

Stephen and Nicole's three-year-old, Sam, always
had trouble going to bed on his own. But after the
birth of his sister, the nighttime stalling escalated

dramatically! Nicole explained: "Now when I say 'night-night' he pleads for 'one more book' . . . 'a glass of water' . . . 'a backrub.' Last night he sobbed that he couldn't stay alone because he could hear bad guys trying to get in the house!"

Tools to Handle Sibling Issues

Here are some easy ways to deal with the problem of sibling competition.

Connect with Respect. Worried kids dig in their heels, especially when they feel rushed. So, when your child is in the throes of anxiety, take a minute to appreciate his feelings with your best Fast-Food Rule + Toddler-ese.

Time-In. A new baby can make an older child feel "kicked off the throne." They often feel like something important has been taken away from them . . . and it has. You can help your child deal with this loss by feeding his meter with many mini time-ins.

Now, more than ever, your older child will love **praise.** Catch him being good throughout the day and be generous with your praise . . . but not *over the top* (don't overdo the jumping up and down and applauding). Use gossip, hand checks, and star charts to encourage the behaviors you like.

Play the Boob. This fun confidence builder helps little kids feel powerful. That's helpful because having a new baby in the house makes toddlers feel that there's a lot over which they have no control. Also, remind your child that the play you enjoy together is "big kid" play and little babies are too tiny and weak to do it.

Before the Baby Arrives

There's a lot you can do to help your older child greet the new baby with love, not jealousy. For example:

- Don't talk too much about the "baby in Mommy's tummy" until two to three months before your due date.
- Give your tot a small doll so he can practice feeding, changing, and good hand washing.
- Let your older child overhear you gossiping to the baby *inside* you (and later, to the baby after birth) about his big sibling's skills and brilliance: "Psst, little baby. I can't wait until David teaches you how to pick up your toys. He can do it superspeedy!"
- Teach your tot patience-stretching and magic breathing so he can practice self-calming before the baby comes and your life gets crazy.
- Be very thoughtful about timing the start of other big changes. Toddlers who are moved from their cribs, made to give up their pacifiers, or put in new schools often feel a little stressed and vulnerable. And if it is done around the time of the new baby, they may even feel betrayed and angry at you and the baby.

  If possible, avoid big changes starting three months before your due date and continuing until six months after the baby's birth (unless your toddler is a *very* secure little guy).
- Buy a great toy that the new baby will "give" to his big brother and have some little toys that you can secretly hand to visitors to your home for them to give your older child for being such a great big brother.

Please set aside any guilty worries about your baby not receiving the same undivided attention from you that your first baby received. What your new baby doesn't get from you, he'll get *five times over* from his big brother or sister.

Routines. Special time and bedtime sweet talk are terrific ways to make your tot feel less jealous. (They're only for "big kids" . . . no babies allowed!) I promise that if you do special time twice a day, this daily investment of ten to twenty minutes will eventually save you hours of nagging and complaints. (Toddlers love getting an occasional *bonus* special time for good cooperation, like going for ice cream!)

Magic Breathing. If your toddler can do it, practice magic breathing every day to help him practice keeping his primitive impulses under control.

Plant Seeds of Kindness. After 18 months, toddlers increasingly want to be good. That's why the arrival of a new child is the perfect time to give lessons in kindness. Let the big sister (or brother) bring you a new diaper when you need one or unpack the grocery bags.

Replace negative comments ("Don't be so rough!") with positive ones. ("Baby loves being touched softly, like this. Hey, you're *good* at that!" Later, gossip to Daddy about the good touching.)

Role-play to let your toddler vent any anger he might feel toward you or the new baby in an acceptable way or to give him a chance to regress a little. ("Do you want to be my baby for a bit? Come sit on my lap, you big strong baby, and you can hug me for a long, long while.")

Behavior Challenge #2: Annoying Attitudes and Actions

As discussed, it's your toddler's job to test the limits, but some just don't know when to quit.

When your toddler dawdles, interrupts, or whines, it can be like fingernails on a chalkboard; you just want it to stop. Many of us are tempted to try to *force* our toddlers to obey with shouts and threats. But often that backfires and makes things worse.

Fortunately, there are several effective ways to reduce annoying behaviors.

Chapter 6 covers the general approach for reducing yellow-light behaviors, but in this next section I'd like to focus on *dawdling* as an example to show how to curb any annoyance (including rudeness, interrupting, whining, back talk, potty mouth, and whatever else drives you bananas!).

Annoying-Behavior Example: Dawdling

Some tots are zippy, but others are slow as snails. Kids who dawdle (delay getting dressed, coming to the table, responding when called) fall into one of two groups:

1. Dreamers—absentminded kids who just get easily distracted.

2. Avoiders—kids who drag things out to avoid doing what's being asked of them.

Tools to Deal with Dawdling

Connect with Respect. Toss out a few phrases of FFR and Toddler-ese to let your child know you can see his point of view (even if you disagree). Then, use a "you-I" sentence (see page 54) to let him know how *you* feel. ("When you don't come I get sad, sad, *sad* . . . because your breakfast gets cold.")

Win-Win Compromise. Next, offer a little fun or a win-win compromise. For example, you might suggest a race: "I'll count to ten and let's see how fast you get your shoes on." Or use a bit of reverse psychology.

> When Jessica delayed and delayed putting her shoes on to prepare for day care, her mom turned toward her daughter's imaginary friend "Nana Mouse" and cupped her hand next to her mouth and gossiped in a loud whisper: "Psst, hey . . . Nana Mouse. Mommy said to put on shoes . . . but Jessie is too little. Jessie cried, 'Waaah, waah! I can't do it!' I guess she is too little to put on shoes all by herself."
>
> In seconds, a grinning Jessica would bounce up and slide into her shoes to prove Mom wrong!

Look for win-win compromises that allow you *both* to "save face."

> Samantha told her three-year-old, Billy, that it was time to leave the park, but her son said he had to fill one more bucket with sand. He then proceeded to put sand in it . . . one grain at a time! Growing impatient, Samantha offered a compromise and then something fun for Billy to look forward to. "You say, 'No, no, no!' You love the park and don't want to leave. But Daddy is waiting. So let's do this. You can put a little more sand in your pail before we leave. Should you take one more minute to put sand in, or two?" Billy quickly said, "Two!" To make it even more fun, Samantha played the boob a little to let Billy feel like an even bigger winner. She said "What!?

> *Two minutes! No way! One is plenty. Okay, you*
> *win. You always win me. You can have two more*
> *minutes. Then as soon as we get home, we can*
> *play ball. . . . I bet I can throw the ball so fast*
> *you'll never catch it! Is that a deal?"*

Remember, when your child keeps his part of the compromise, always reward him with a tiny time-in (like a hug, some praise, gossip, a bit of play) or playing the boob.

However, if your child doesn't cooperate (or if you have no time for respectful listening and little compromises), then it's time for a mild consequence like clap-growl or kind ignoring.

Kind Ignoring. Since annoying acts are yellow-light behaviors ("I don't like that.") not red-light ones ("Stop now!"), they can usually be handled with just a little "cold shoulder."

Here's how you might put all these steps together for an annoying behavior, like whining:

> *"You really, really, really want a cookie. But that*
> *whiny voice hurts my ears. So Mommy has to go*
> *away for a second. But as soon as you use your*
> *'happy' voice, I'll come right back and you can*
> *tell me what you want."*

Then turn your back and pretend to be busy doing something on the other side of the room (don't look back). Ignore any increase in whining, but as soon as your little friend uses his nice voice, reward him by immediately returning and offering a cheerful comment: "*That's* the voice my ears like!" Then you can choose what to offer: 1) a cookie, 2) a cookie, only *after* he picks up his toys, 3) respectful sympathy but no more cookies for now.

If, however, the kind ignoring doesn't work and the annoying behaviors cross the line into unbearable, that's when you need to count to three and use a "take-control" consequence like time-out or giving a fine.

Bernadette was having a pokey morning and wouldn't get dressed for the park . . . even though she loved playing outside. So her dad, Alvin, said, "Get dressed before the dinger rings or we won't have time to play in the park." Then he turned his back for a few seconds to see what she would do next.

Had she started getting dressed, he would have praised her and helped her along. But instead she continued to dawdle. So Alvin decided to play the boob. He pretended to "help" her get dressed, but kept making silly mistakes like trying to put her pants on over her head and saying in a boastful, boobish way, "Yes! Yes! That's how they go! I'm sure of it . . . right?"

Unfortunately, she dug in her heels and just refused to put on her clothes. So Alvin decided to give Bernadette a fine for dawdling too long. "You really, really don't want to get dressed. Okay. No problem," he stated matter-of-factly, "but then, no park today . . . maybe tomorrow." And with that he turned his back and left.

Five minutes later Bernadette announced she was ready to go, and Alvin calmly replied, "I know you love the park, but you waited sooo long today, there is no time." Bernadette had a meltdown and cried, and Alvin lovingly acknowledged her disappointment and offered

her some juice. When she pouted and refused,
he did a minute of kind ignoring and she
stopped her complaints.

 The next day, when her dad offered to take
her to the park, he suggested a little "getting
dressed" race: "I bet you can't get dressed by the
time I count to ten!" And she got dressed
superfast. "Wow!" he exclaimed. "You got
dressed as fast as a jet plane . . . zoooom!"

Put Annoying Behaviors "On Hold"

A great way to stop your child from becoming a "profes-
sional whiner" is to put his behavior "on hold." Just to remind you, this is when you *almost* give your child what he's
begging for; then at the last moment you turn and pretend
you suddenly have to do something else for a minute.
Please reread page 172. . . . This one is worth its weight in
gold!

Simple Steps to *Prevent* Annoying Behavior

Even better than *stopping* nagging and whining is *preventing*
them. You can do this by using the same approach recom-
mended for preventing tantrums (see page 224):

1) Avoid problem situations.

2) Connect with respect . . . all day long.

3) Feed the meter.

4) Teach patience-stretching and magic breathing.

The Old Switcheroo: Getting Tots to Take Their Medicine

Lots of children resist taking their medicine. And trying to force them to swallow it down can lead to power struggles, wasted medicine, and a stressed-out family.

But here's one little technique that really gets the job done for older toddlers . . . even though it's a tiny bit sneaky and involves giving a smidge of soda. Here's what you do:

Before giving your toddler his medicine, pour about an ounce of decaffeinated, dark-colored soda (like root beer) into each of two small glasses. Next, mix a dose of medicine into one of the glasses. (You can also try dark grape juice, but a strong-flavored, fizzy soda works best to hide bitterness.)

Now call your toddler, and while he watches put his medicine in a spoon and say, "Take this, sweetie, then you can have a little soda. Some soda for you and some for me." If he willingly takes his medicine give him the *plain* soda . . . and a pat on the back. (A little later, gossip to his teddy about how he swallowed down all of his medicine and made you happy.)

If your child refuses the medicine, repeat your offer: "Take this really fast, sweetheart, then you can have your yummy soda." Play the boob by begging a little (ham it up): "Please take it. *P-l-e-a-s-e!!!*" If he refuses again, pout and say, "Okay, *you* win! You *always* win! I *never* get to win! Here's your soda," *but* hand him the glass that's *mixed with the medicine.* Your toddler will guzzle the soda—and medicine—fast. He'll be in such a hurry to drink it down before you change your mind, he'll never realize he's been hoodwinked!

Don't gloat or say, "Gotcha!" when it's over. That may make your little one feel tricked and cause him to refuse the soda when the next dose is due. After the soda/medicine combo is taken, show your child that you're pouring the spoon of medicine back into the bottle and set him free again.

Behavior Challenge #3: Defiance

All little kids defy their parents from time to time. Sometimes it's because the thrill of doing something "forbidden" is *irresistible,* or it's *payback* for being stopped from doing something he wanted to do earlier in the day, or perhaps he has just forgotten the rule. But regardless of the reason, defiance can push our buttons like nothing else. We get mad, then *our* emotional elevator drops down, down, down to a primitive state of anger. Too often, we get sucked in so fast we just react . . . and then overreact.

Note: To help put a stop to this process before you react explosively, it's a good idea for *you* to practice magic breathing! When you have a calm moment, sit comfortably, relax your face, and take a few deep breaths—slow in and slow out—to help you practice staying in control of your emotions.

The Silver Lining of Your Little Tot's Defiance

Think of defiance as a sign of *courage* . . . the ability to stand up for oneself. It was gutsy of our ancient ancestors to fight off wild animals with just rocks and sticks, and it's gutsy for toddlers to resist parents who are five times their size!

Of course, I'm not saying we should encourage defiance. But I do believe the goal is to get our headstrong toddlers to *join the team* . . . not to break their spirits.

A little defiance is normal, but repeated disrespect must be stopped. Now here's the tricky part: Trying to squash your child's defiance with a display of anger often boomerangs. (Think of it as trying to intimidate a member of a motorcycle gang!) Rather than meekly giving in, your macho (or macha) little friend may actually yell right in your face and refuse to back down.

Tools to *Prevent* Defiance

In a moment, I'll talk about *stopping* defiance. But first, here are some simple steps to *prevent* it before it happens.

Feed the Meter. Throughout a normal, happy day, offer your child *dozens* of little time-ins (like attention, praise, gossip, and hand checks), fun routines (like special time), and confidence builders (like offering options and playing the boob) to make him feel like a winner. These steps build the loving bond and magically help our kids become more cooperative and less defiant.

Practice Patience-Stretching and Magic Breathing. When you teach your child self-control you'll make it easier for him to avoid conflict—with you or anyone else.

Plant Seeds of Kindness. Practice by role-playing, by telling homespun fairy tales with messages about life lessons regarding right and wrong, and by catching others being good.

Tools to *Stop* Defiance

You will be most successful teaching your children respect, fairness, and calmness when you model them yourself, during times of conflict.

So when you're caught in a toddler rebellion, use your *ambassadorial* skills to help you turn conflict into cooperation. Here's how:

Connect with Respect. Use a few phrases to show you understand and care.

Let Your Child "Save Face." To help both you and your toddler save face, try offering options, inventing little competitions (making a game out of what you are requesting, like having a race), or suggesting a win-win compromise:

Offer Options

> Three-year-old Selma hates getting dressed in the morning, so her mother has learned how to offer her options that yield the desired result: "Selma, you really, really don't want to get dressed. You love just playing with your toys. I'm so, so sorry, but Mommy has to leave very soon, so here's your choice: You can dress yourself or I can take you to the store in your pajamas (even though you might get cold). Which one sounds best, get dressed or be in your cold pajamas?"

Play (Make it a game)

> Sofia wasn't a big eater, so her mother, Agapi, wanted her daughter to at least drink some milk to take in a little protein and calcium. This was usually a big struggle. One day Agapi's sister suggested she sidestep the conflict by making it into a little race. Agapi decided to give it a try.
> The next day, when Agapi put the milk in front of her strong-willed two-year-old, she

said, "I'll count to five and see if you can finish your milk." Sofia smiled and drank half and Agapi encouraged her to drink down a little more. "Wow! You drank that superfast! I'll count to five again and see if you can finish it all . . . but please save one little drop for me. Pleease! Okay? On your mark . . . get set . . . go!" Sophia drank it all, not even leaving a drop. To keep up the fun, Agapi added a bit of playing the boob and in a pretend whine said, "No fair! You drank MY milk too!" Sofia flashed her a grin a mile wide.

Win-Win Compromise

Four-year-old Ben loved the park and ignored his mom's calls to stop playing. So she knelt down next to him and acknowledged his feelings:

"You are having so much fun! You love, love the park! You don't even want to come when I call. You just want to play, play, play!"

Then, when Ben looked up, his mom saw it was now her turn to give a message and she offered a win-win compromise: "But we have to go make some yummy dinner, sweetheart. So here's your choice: We can leave now and play football at home, or you can play here for two more minutes. Your choice, sweetheart, fun football at home or two minutes here?"

If defiance continues, it's time for a consequence:

Mild Consequence. For mild defiance, do a clap-growl or connect with respect plus kind ignoring.

Arianna found herself constantly having to nag three-year-old Morgan to get ready for school. When she learned *The Happiest Toddler* approach, she decided to give it a try. The next time her daughter refused to put on her shoes, Arianna responded by connecting with respect and then adding a little kind ignoring: "You say, 'No, no, no! No shoes!' I know you don't want to put them on, honey, but you know what no shoes means: no play outside. So Mommy will be right back to see if you're ready for your shoes. And then we can also eat your crunchy cereal."

Arianna turned her back for twenty seconds and pretended to be straightening up some papers at the other end of the room. She then returned and repeated, "Come on, sweetheart. Let's put on shoes so you can eat your crunchies and play!" Morgan protested, "No, I want my crunchies *now!*"

Then her mom did a very smart thing. Rather than getting into a fight, she tried the technique of putting her "on hold" (see page 172). Arianna said, "Okay, honey, you win. Here are your crunchies." But just as she was putting the cereal on the table she abruptly stopped and said, "Wait! Wait! I almost forgot. Where are your shoes, you silly goose? Superquick, get your shoes . . . then let's have some yummy crunchies!" And she turned and again pretended to be busy for twenty seconds.

Arianna ignored Morgan as she protested, "I want my crunchies." And then, with a big pout

on her face, she suddenly got up and brought her
shoes to her mom to be put on. Arianna
immediately rewarded her daughter's
cooperation with an enthusiastic cheer and by
offering her an option of cereal bowls: "Yea!
Good job! Now, would you like your crunchies in
the dinosaur bowl or in the blue cup?"

"Take-Charge" Consequence. For serious disrespect, do a clap-growl (to show your displeasure) and then use a time-out or give a fine.

Remember, your child is leaving you no choice but to give a consequence. "You are forcing me to give you a time-out." After the time-out, *don't* immediately talk about her defiance. Wait until later that day to gossip about how her actions made you unhappy or role-play about it with her dolls.

Defiant-Behavior Example: Resisting the Car Seat

At 15 months, Henry began to squirm and fuss
when Patrice went to buckle him into the car
seat. "You have to have the harness on; it's
important to keep you safe," his mom would
explain. But Henry just fought and wriggled.
Patrice said, "Some days, belting him in is like
wrestling a greased pig!"

Young toddlers hate being confined. They often resist getting in car seats, sitting still on the bus, putting on party clothes, etc. You can try to reason them out of their resistance, but what if your loving logic just doesn't work?

Tools to Prevent Car-Seat Fights

Here are a few ways to prevent car-seat conflicts before they happen:

Practice. Put the car seat in the living room and have him sit in it while you give him a minute of time-in (snack, read, etc.). Once he accepts the car seat at home, start going for very short rides (just around the block). Reward his cooperation with a time-in. Soon your tyke will learn that car seats are no big deal. Don't forget to gossip about his cooperation (to his stuffed animals, Grandma, or anybody). Paste photos of your child happily sitting in his car seat into a little book ("My Car Seat" scrapbook) and view it with him at bedtime to remind him of the fun things he does when he's in his car seat.

Catch Others Being Good. Point out when you see other kids in their car seats. Cut pictures of happy kids sitting in their car seats from magazines and add them to the scrapbook. Let your child overhear you gossip about the car-seat cooperation of kids he knows.

Fairy Tales. For older car-seat resisters, making up stories about giving in will plant the seed of cooperation and may help you prevent the conflict from ever occurring:

> Charlie the Crab hated to be in the car
> seat . . . but he loved swimming with the other
> crabs at the clear, blue lake. He was sooo crabby.
> "No seat! No seat!" he'd cry over and over! But
> one day his friend Finny the Fish told him, "Hey,
> Charlie, when I was little I didn't like car seats,
> but now my mom sings songs with me and we

sing the whole way to the lake. It's fun! What's
your favorite song? Let's sing it now!"

Role-Play. Play with his dolls and his car seat. Have one
doll be the child who resists the seat and another doll be the
mommy who says, "I know you hate it, little dolly. You say,
'No, no, *no!*' But let's have some fun and make it your *fun
seat*! We can sing a silly song or read a book . . . your choice."

Tools to End a Car-Seat Fight

If the struggle has already begun, try this:

Connect with Respect. Even when you have to enforce a
rule, remember to show your respect:

> At least twice a week, Christianne's 29-month-
> old firecracker, Aurora, would erupt into
> screaming in the middle of a car ride.
> Christianne couldn't stop, but she tried her best
> to let her little one know she really got her
> message. " 'No, no, no!' You say, 'No car, Mommy.
> No, no, no!!' " She would vigorously wave one
> arm, wag her finger and say, "You hate it, hate it!
> You say, 'No, no, no!' "

When you find yourself in this situation, repeatedly echo
your child's feelings and aim for his sweet spot. It may not
stop his crying, but it will make him feel understood and respected, and it will help him recover faster once you get
home. (Wait until a quiet time, much later, to give your lecture about the dangers of cars and why car seats are smart to
use.)

Win-Win Compromise. Offer a win-win compromise to show respect and gain cooperation.

> *Three-year-old Baron often complained that his car seat was "too tight." But his dad used his love of music to find a compromise. "I'm so sorry, Baron, but Daddy has to put you in the seat. I know you really, really hate it, very much! But wait, wait! I have a very important question. Do you want me to put on your Silly Songs music before you sit in the seat or after?"*

Gossip. After you get back home, let your child overhear you gossiping about his struggles and successes.

> *"Psst! Hey, Elmo! Moses didn't like his car seat at first and started to cry. But then we started to sing the Happy Birthday song and he got happy and became a super-duper car-seat sitter! I'm gonna tell Daddy what a good job he did!"*

Defiant-Behavior Example: Picky Eating

> *"Dr. Karp, I swear he lives on air. He eats one cracker and that's it for the day!"*
> —Shana, mom of two-year-old Danny

Feeding, feeding, feeding has been your big job for a long, long time. We all feel like good parents when our kids clean their plates.

Yet many toddlers tenaciously refuse any food other than crackers, macaroni and cheese, and buttered bread. Don't take this fussiness personally; it's just a normal part of the rigidity so common to the toddler years. Take some time to read a book or check with your doctor to learn the amount of nutrients your child really needs, and track his food intake over a week or two to see if he is getting enough. Most kids require less than we think.

Tools to Handle Picky Eaters

Smart parents avoid battles they can't win. So rather than trying to force your child to eat something he doesn't want, sidestep the conflict by hiding it in the food he likes or finding a win-win compromise.

Connect with Respect. Narrate your child's strong desire not to eat so she knows you understand.

Catch Others Being Good. Point out what kids have on their plates when you visit restaurants. Invite older kids to your house to eat a meal. Toddlers love imitating others, especially slightly older kids.

Win-Win Compromise. Compete to see who can chomp down the "little trees" (broccoli) the fastest. Offer choices ("Should I give you three peas or two?") and suggest a win-win compromise ("Eat a green bean and you can have another French fry. Eat two more green beans and you can have all five of these French fries!"). If your toddler drives a hard bargain and eats only one tiny nibble of the bean, you should still give her a piece of the French fry because that's definitely a baby step in the right direction.

Reverse Psychology. When your toddler reaches for a piece of broccoli, at first let her have only a tiny piece. Say, "No way! Mommy wants them ALL. . . . They're Mommy's trees." When your tot gobbles up her piece, make a silly pout and say, "Hey, you ate *my* broccoli!!"

> When two-year-old Celia refused to eat, Mark
> and Karen pretended to try to sneak bits of food
> off her plate as though they were greedy and
> wanted all her food for themselves.
>   "We appeal to her basic sense of 'It's mine!' "
> says Mark. "It works about half the time, but a
> 50-50 success rate ain't so bad."

Putting Bad Behavior "On Hold." Lips still zipped? If your child still won't eat, let her leave the table. However, if she returns for a little milk or sweets, you might put her "on hold" by doing something like this:

Begin to hand her the milk, then suddenly stop and offer her a *smidge* of dinner first. "You want milky? Okay, sweetheart, here's your milk. Oops, silly Mommy! Mommy forgot, big girls have to eat one green bean before milky! Do you want to eat this big one or this little teeny, tiny, baby bean?"

If she refuses, say, "No problem, my love. But no beans . . . no milky." Then say, "I'll check on you in just a sec to see if you're ready for your bean." Now turn and busy yourself with something for thirty seconds. Then turn back and whisper, "I know you don't like beans sooooooo much. So should we find a teeny, tiny one or would you rather just eat a half of one?"

As soon as she eats her bean, reward her with a smile, milk, and a little time-in. This will encourage faster cooperation in the future.

Be a Master of Disguise

Okay, the following may sound like you are being a spy more than an ambassador, but here are my favorite tricks for getting nutrients and veggies past your toddler's lips:

- Appeal to her "sour tooth." Cut vegetables into French fry–size strips, cook them, then marinate them overnight in pickle juice or Italian dressing.
- Blend veggies into a soup.
- Blend and bake veggies into batter bread. Use a recipe for zucchini bread, but use pureed broccoli in place of zucchini and double the amount the recipe calls for.
- Make yam chips by baking or broiling them in an oven with a little salt and butter.
- Dip lightly steamed veggies into ranch or creamy Italian dressing.
- Grind zucchini or carrots and put them into pancakes and serve them with syrup.
- Serve fresh carrot or carrot/apple juice.

- Iron is important for blood, muscle, and brain growth. You can add a lot of iron to your child's diet just by cooking in a cast-iron pot or skillet. Add lemon juice or vinegar and the acid will really help bring the iron out of the metal and into the food.

- Your toddler needs 12 mg. of iron a day. Iron-rich foods include black beans (1 cup has 8 mg.), liver (4 oz. has 7.9 mg.), lentils (1 cup has 6.6 mg.), beef (4 oz. has 3.6 mg.), blackstrap molasses (1 tablespoon has 3.5 mg.), raisins (8 oz. has 3.2 mg.), prune juice (8 oz. has 3 mg.), or cooked greens (½ cup of mustard greens, dandelion greens, or collards has 2.6 mg.). Squeeze a little lemon juice over iron-rich foods—you'll increase iron absorption severalfold. (But dark grape juice cuts iron absorption by over 50 percent.)

- Your toddler needs 700 to 1,000 mg. of calcium each day. Some powerhouse sources of calcium that are easy to sneak into your toddler's diet include skim milk powder, which is easy to mix into foods (2 oz. contains 400 mg.); blackstrap molasses (1 tablespoon has 290 mg.); sesame seed butter (tahini), sold in health-food stores (2 oz. has 270 mg.); yogurt (8 oz. has 270 mg.); grated Parmesan (2 oz. has 260 mg.); and broccoli (1 stalk has 160 mg.). And you can give your child a further calcium boost simply by letting her play outside! Just fifteen to thirty minutes of sunlight a day will help her body make vitamin D, which is essential for her to fully benefit from the calcium in her diet. (Don't forget to put on the sunscreen if your toddler is going to be out in the sun for more than thirty minutes.)

Behavior Challenge #4: Aggressive and/or Dangerous Behavior

Up until now in this chapter we've been talking about dealing with yellow-light behaviors. But, this last group of parental challenges is made up of red-light behaviors. *You* get to go first

("Stop now!") when your tot's acts are violent or dangerous. These acts demand immediate action. Once the behavior has stopped, *then* you can spend a minute reflecting his feelings.

The kids who are most aggressive are those who:

- have spirited, high-energy temperaments
- are extra impulsive and distractible
- are under extra stress
- don't speak well
- are bored, cooped up, lonely, or stressed

If your tot is a wild child, there's a lot you can do to prevent his repeated acts of aggression. As mentioned earlier, you'll be able to dramatically reduce the fighting and cut the number of time-outs simply by boosting your child's time-ins!

However, when it's too late to *prevent* a problem, then it's time for you to jump in with some clear and consistent consequences.

Dangerous-Behavior Example: Sibling Aggression

Twins Caleb and Elijah, 24 months old, were playing nicely at the sandbox in the park two blocks from their apartment. Suddenly, Caleb decided he wanted the sand-sifter Elijah was using. He reached for it, but Elijah quickly yanked it away. In retaliation, Caleb whacked his brother's head with his shovel . . . and Elijah promptly whacked him right back!

In a flash, their father, Alan, clapped and growled, scooped them up, and carried them out of the park. Once home, he immediately put them both in time-out.

Your toddler's veneer of civilization is so thin it doesn't take much to propel him back to his primitive nature: hitting, poking, pinching, whacking, biting. (More about biting in the next section.) And, having *two* little cave-kids to supervise can make you feel more like a boxing referee than a parent.

Tools to Handle Sibling Fights

Here are two straightforward ways to get control:

Connect with Respect. Upset toddlers are usually the most emotional people in the room and that's why we generally acknowledge *their* feelings before we give *our* message. But in red-light situations, *we* get to go first. "Stop! No hit! No hit! We *don't* hit people." Only *after* the danger or aggression stops do we use the Fast-Food Rule and Toddler-ese to narrate our toddler's anger or frustration.

"Take-Charge" Consequence. When your kids are fighting, it may be obvious to you which one deserves a time-out. But if you're not sure who the chief culprit is, it's often best to discipline *both* kids. I know that may seem a little unfair, but here's why it can be the right thing to do: First, it's often hard to know who the victim really is (sometimes, the munchkin you thought was innocent actually provoked the fight by teasing or taunting), and second, it teaches that regardless of who started the fight, they both have responsibility for having continued it.

Later in the day, use your other tools (like gossip, role-play, fairy tales, catching others being good, etc.) to encourage anything positive about the fight (like stopping when you said "Stop!") and to discourage what you disliked (like biting or using hurtful words).

Kids who get into lots of fights may need more time to run around outside. They often benefit from attending nursery school to keep them busy and out of mischief.

When to Step Back . . . and Let Your Kids Solve It

You don't necessarily have to intervene in every *slugfest* your kids have. Small struggles help kids learn to stand up for themselves and be courageous. Besides, sooner or later, you will want your kids to learn to settle their differences on their own.

So as long as the fight is a yellow-light situation, not a red-light one (that is, it involves bickering and bellowing, but not bleeding), let the kids struggle a bit before you intervene. When you enter the room, use the Fast-Food Rule and Toddler-ese to show you understand that they're *both* upset and that you really care. Then excuse yourself and give them another minute to work it out. (Of course, if the fighting spins out of control—physically or verbally—it's time to step in and hand out some consequences.)

Dangerous-Behavior Example: Biting

Biting is a common behavior for primitive cave-kids. They typically chomp during teething or when frustrated. But if this behavior is not discouraged, promptly and powerfully, it can turn into a dangerous habit (like biting other kids' faces or biting babies).

> *Just as Monica finished tying her 16-month-old's shoe, he bit her shoulder—hard! "Owww!" Monica yelped. Then, struggling to compose herself, she scolded him lovingly, mildly, "Please, Lukie! That's not nice. Mommy doesn't like biting."*

Do you think Lucas stopped? Nope! In fact, he soon began biting whenever he got mad.

Tools to Deal with Biting

Here's how to stop this dangerous behavior fast:

Consequences. If the chomper bites before you can stop him, he needs a consequence. With a young toddler, start with a mild consequence.

Clap-Growl. In the example above, Monica's message, "Mommy doesn't like biting," failed to work because it was way too sweet. Remember, in emotional situations, what you say is much less important than the way you say it. Be firm and wear a serious expression to match.

If you happen to see your tot open his mouth right as he's about to nip, give some fast, hard claps, make a deep, menacing growl, do a double take (page 178), and with a warning finger held up, bark, "Hey . . . *hey*!! No bite. *No* bite!!"

Don't stare at your child after the warning. Staring may make a defiant kid disobey even more!

Kind Ignoring. Immediately remove your little biter from the situation. Give him a "cold shoulder" for twenty to thirty seconds and lavish some sympathy on the child who was nipped. (Let the biter overhear you gossip to his victim, "I say, 'No, no, *no!*' I don't like it when Lukie bites. Kids have to use their words when they're mad. I like it when kids who are really angry say, 'No, no! I don't like it!' ") After a minute or two of kind ignoring, reengage your child with a little friendly talking or play.

Later in the day, gossip to his teddy bear about how you don't like biting. Role-play the incident and ask your child what the "biter" could do to make the bitten doll feel better. You might also tell a fairy tale. Perhaps a little story about the girl bunny who was sad because she would bite so much that the other bunnies didn't want to play with her. So her mommy taught her a special trick: Every time she wanted to bite, she should show her teeth and click them together three times . . . but never bite. The other little bunnies thought this was funny and then they all wanted to play with her! This made her smile and she lived happily ever after. The end!

"Take-Charge" Consequence. Children who bite hard or are "repeat offenders" get an immediate consequence, like a mini time-out (page 194), time-out, or a fine.

Dangerous-Behavior Example: Running Away from You

One last dangerous behavior you may have to deal with is when your child darts away from you in a crowded mall or parking lot. Obviously, running away in public is totally unacceptable and must be stopped immediately.

Tools to Stop Children Who Run Away

In red-light situations, there is just no time to respectfully acknowledge your child's feelings. When there's a danger or your child is breaking an important family rule . . . *you* get to go first!

Clap-Growl. Give a loud clap and growl then demand, "No! *Stop!* Now!" You may have to raise your voice, or you may be able to get his attention with a stern voice and frown. (If your child doesn't stop immediately and you have to run after him, keep a serious face so he doesn't confuse this with a game of chase.)

Connect with Respect. Once your child is safe, *then* it's his turn to have his feelings validated:

"You wanted the ball. You said, 'Kick ball!' You ran, ran, ran . . . but nooo! No street, *no*! Cars! Cars hurt kids! *Ouch!*"

If your child tries to run away again, it's time for an immediate consequence. (See page 200 for a way to give a time-out when you are away from home.)

Epilogue

Civilization Ho!
Your Happy,
Confident
Four-Year-Old

"The journey is the reward."

—Taoist saying

Congratulations! You've just guided your toddler through some of the most amazing, fast-paced, challenging developments she'll experience in her entire life!

She has been miraculously transformed from a one-year-old (gleefully practicing her first steps and words), to an 18-month-old (swaggering with the new thrill of freedom and falling prey to wild emotional swings), to a two-year-old (learning the simple rules of language and social cooperation), to a three-year-old (fascinated by people, play, art, humor, and friendship), to a four-year-old (a budding expert in art, humor, and making friends).

Whew! No wonder this has been such an exhausting period for all of you! And now here you are on the brink of your child's fifth birthday. Soon you'll be leaving toddlerhood

behind as your child knocks at the gates of childhood to begin her long life as a citizen of the civilized world.

Of course, there is still a lot of work ahead, but your beautiful child is no longer a little primitive. Five-year-olds are ready for all sorts of exciting new cultural experiences, like writing, reading, Little League, and lemonade stands.

And if you thought toddlerhood was amazing, just wait. Over the next couple of years, your child's sense of humor will blossom (Uh-oh . . . barf and poop jokes are coming!), her curiosity about the world will explode ("Why? Why? Why?"), and she'll fall madly in love with her friends ("But Mommy, I have to go to Mary's party! *Please!?*").

Your child's development and maturation don't mean she'll totally outgrow *The Happiest Toddler* parenting lessons. Of course, you'll use growling a lot less (although you may be tempted to bring it back during the teen years), but the basic tools, like the Fast-Food Rule, feeding the meter, and win-win compromises, will serve you well through *all* the years of your little one's childhood. Truthfully, none of us ever outgrows the need to hear our feelings heard, understood, and respected.

And don't expect to throw Toddler-ese away in a dumpster the minute your little friend blows out her four birthday candles. As the years pass, you'll no longer be jabbing your finger in the air exclaiming, "*You* want! *You* want!" But you will still be using shorter phrases and repetition, and mirroring a bit of your child's feelings to help soothe her emotional upsets, for many more years. (Remember, even adults slide down an emotional elevator when we're distraught, and we feel most heard if our friends and loved ones manage to hit our sweet spot when they acknowledge our feelings.)

I hope you'll look back fondly on these happy toddler days. Once you're past this period, you'll have a bit of a breather. The next ten years will also have unique challenges, but you will have mastered the most important skills you'll ever need to be a great parent.

Congratulations, have fun, and hold on! As fast as toddlerhood passes, the years of childhood will rocket by even faster!

Appendix A

The Ten Basics for Raising a Happy Toddler

1. **It helps to think of your toddler as a little caveman.**
   With all their grunting and grabbing, toddlers can act uncivilized. In fact, their brains are actually pretty primitive and out of balance. The part that's good at language and logic is immature, and the part that's emotional and impulsive is in the driver's seat. Even our brains lose much of their language and logic ability when we're upset (we get so mad we "go ape!"). But since toddlers are primitive to start with, when they're upset their brains get so stressed-out they seem to go . . . *prehistoric*!

2. **Know your toddler's temperament.**
   Is your child laid-back? Cautious? Spirited? Knowing your toddler's temperament will help you be better at anticipating his needs and reactions so you can be a better parent.

3. Give yourself a pat on the back. Parenting is hard.
Parenting is a challenging job. Besides having to
handle your primitive little pal's ups and downs,
you'll regularly have to struggle with these common
parenting problems:

■ *You don't have enough help:* If you're like most
parents today, you don't have the rich network of
family and friends that parents throughout history have relied on to help them at home. And
at the same time, you may be struggling with a
modern challenge that past generations rarely
encountered: Dads *and* Moms having to leave
the home to hold down full-time jobs.

■ *You feel like a flop:* Most new parents have no
training and little experience. No wonder we feel
demoralized when our little Bamm-Bamms do
the normal things that all toddlers do: have
meltdowns, act unreasonably, and challenge the
rules.

■ *Your buttons get pushed:* Don't be surprised if
your toddler's spitting and shrieks unexpectedly
awaken within you painful memories or upsetting feelings from deep in your past.

■ *You have a personality mismatch:* Does your personality clash with your little one's? If so, take a
breath, count your blessings, and focus on what
you love about your child.

4. Be an *ambassador* to your uncivilized little tot.
Once you realize your toddler is uncivilized (especially when she's mad), it becomes clear why parenting is so tricky. Most successful moms and dads
handle their toddler's upsets with a mix of respect,

kindness, and diplomatic limit setting. In other words, you'll be the most successful if you think of yourself *not* as your child's "boss" or "buddy," but as a skillful *ambassador* from the 21st century to your primitive little friend.

5. **Practice the *Fast-Food Rule* every day.**
Upset toddlers often get so frantic they seem deaf to our calm words of explanation and reason. That's why, when your tot is tantrumming, it's *imperative* that you spend a minute echoing what you think she wants and feels—to help her settle down a bit—before taking a turn to tell her *your* important message.

6. **Speak in your upset toddler's native lingo—*Toddler-ese*.**
Toddlers aren't that good with language to begin with, and when they're upset, their stressed-out brains struggle with our words even more. That's why when your child is emotional—mad, sad, scared, etc.—she'll understand you the best if you translate your statements into a simpler style of language, *Toddler-ese*. It's as easy as one-two-three:
1) Use short phrases.
2) Repeat the phrases several times.
3) Use animated gestures and an expressive tone of voice to mirror a bit of your child's feeling. That allows you to connect with her emotional *sweet spot*.

7. **Encourage your child's good (*green-light*) behavior with lots of fun interactions like:**

- **Time-ins:** Lavish your child with tiny bits of *attention, play, praise, gossip, hand checks,* et cetera, at least twenty times a day.
- **Confidence builders:** Make your child feel like a winner by offering choices and *playing the boob* whenever you can.
- **Teaching patience:** Increase your child's control over her outbursts by practicing *patience-stretching* and *magic breathing.*
- **Routines:** Create fun routines like *bedtime sweet talk* and *special time* to help your tot feel smart, happy, and loved.
- **Planting seeds of kindness:** Teach your child how to be kind and considerate by means of: 1) *fairy tales,* 2) *catching others being good,* 3) *role-playing.*

8. **Curb your child's annoying (*yellow-light*) behaviors.**

   All toddlers dawdle, whine, and defy, but you can curb these annoyances by *connecting with respect* (a combination of the *Fast-Food Rule + Toddler-ese*), by offering *win-win compromises* to encourage better behavior, and by giving *mild consequences* (like *clap-growl* or *kind ignoring*) when the nuisance continues.

9. **Put a quick halt to your child's unacceptable (*red-light*) behaviors.**

   When your child is aggressive, doing something dangerous, or breaking a key family rule, it's time for you to stop the situation fast with a *"take-charge"* consequence (*time-out* or *giving a fine*).

10. **Prevent most tantrums or lovingly stop them in their tracks.**

You can stop half of your toddler's tantrums in seconds just by using the *Fast-Food Rule + Toddler-ese*. And, even more amazingly, you can prevent 50 to 90 percent of toddler outbursts from ever happening by: avoiding problem situations, *connecting with respect* all day long, *feeding the meter* (with frequent *time-ins, playing the boob, routines,* etc.), and teaching *patience-stretching*.

Appendix B

Dr. Karp's Key Terms and All-Star Tricks!

There are so many *Happiest Toddler* parenting tips and skills, I've included this short glossary to help you remember the ones you'll be using the most:

Avoid problem situations
Prevent tantrums by avoiding common tantrum triggers, such as fatigue, hunger, caffeine, boredom, aggressive or violent videos, TV, etc. (page 225).

Bedtime sweet talk
A nightly routine that reminds your child of the many good things she did that day and previews some of the fun things she can look forward to the next day (page 129).

Catch others being good

Point out to your child other children and adults who are demonstrating the actions and attitudes you want to encourage in her (page 142).

Clap-growl

Several loud claps followed by a low growl is both a warning signal and a mild consequence that all cave-kids understand (page 176).

Confidence builders

Little self-esteem boosters that make your toddler feel like a winner (such as asking your child's opinion and playing the boob) (page 113).

Connect with respect

This is talking to your upset child using the Fast-Food Rule spoken in your very best Toddler-ese (page 150).

Double take

After you get your toddler's attention with a clap-growl, put up a finger and turn your face away for a moment. This shows that you're the boss and helps avoid getting into staring matches (page 178).

Fairy tales

Like the age-old tradition of teaching values through storytelling, these are little stories that you make up to illustrate a specific lesson you want your child to learn (page 138).

Fast-Food Rule

Before telling an upset person *your* point of view, first repeat back how he's feeling . . . in a way that touches the sweet spot of his emotions (page 41).

Feed the meter
Giving your tot many bits of fun and attention all day long is an almost instantaneous way to boost her good behavior (page 97).

Give a fine
Removing a valued privilege or possession is a way to punish unacceptable behaviors (page 202).

Give in fantasy
When you can't or won't give your child something she wants, tell her how you *wish* you could give it to her . . . and much, much more (page 154).

Gossip
Supersize the impact of your praise (or criticism) by letting your child overhear you whispering it to someone else, like Daddy, a bird on the lawn, or his favorite teddy bear (page 104).

Green-light behavior
Good things your child says and does that you want to praise and encourage (page 95).

Hand check
Little pen marks you put on the back of your child's hand when she does good deeds. They're a terrific way to make her feel good about herself all day long (page 107).

Kind ignoring
Discourage annoying yellow-light behaviors (like whining and dawdling) by briefly turning your back to deprive your tot of your attention (page 180).

Lovey

A cuddly "companion"—like a silky blanket or stuffed animal—that your toddler can snuggle with for comfort and reassurance (page 135).

Magic breathing

Deep breathing helps toddlers to develop self-control and reduce stress (page 125).

Mild consequences

Small consequences (clap-growl, kind ignoring) used to curb annoying yellow-light behaviors (page 175).

Patience-stretching

An instantly effective way to help even young toddlers learn how to control their impulses and wait patiently (page 122).

Plant seeds of kindness

Encourage the development of your tot's character through the "side door" of his mind by mentioning the values you want to see rather than telling your child what to do (page 137).

Play the boob

A confidence builder. This all-time favorite parenting trick makes your tot feel strong and smart by making you seem a little silly, slow, and klutzy (page 116).

Praise

Let your child know you like what she's doing by giving her a balanced diet of praise. Throughout the day, mix a bit of "applause" with a bunch of compliments and a whole lot of gentle, smiling approval (page 102).

Put bad behavior "on hold"
A way to use patience-stretching to sidestep your child's whining and demands and teach him to be more reasonable (page 172).

Red-light behavior
Things your child says or does that are dangerous or aggressive or that violate important family rules and that you need to stop . . . immediately (page 185).

Reverse psychology
A clever way to get your child to do something by ordering him *not* to do it (page 174).

Role-playing
A playful way to give your child the opportunity to practice behaviors you want to encourage (page 143).

Saving face
Shaming or embarrassing your toddler may lead to resentment and actually *decrease* cooperation. Saving face means allowing him to keep his dignity, even when he doesn't get his way (page 160).

Show your tot you believe in him
This is a confidence builder in which you ask for your child's help, offer him options, or give him a minute to figure things out for himself (page 115).

Side door of your child's mind
Toddlers learn more from indirect messages—fairy tales, role-playing, and catching others being good—than from lectures and long explanations. Their natural tendency is to

imitate what they see and overhear (through the "side door" of the mind) rather than what they're told to do (page 137).

Special time

A daily routine of one to two short (five- to ten-minute) sessions of uninterrupted fun and attention. It's a *gift* that many kids fondly remember for the rest of their lives (page 133).

Spokesperson

A method of acknowledging your child's feelings by saying what you think she would if she could (page 76).

Sportscaster

A method of acknowledging your child's feelings by narrating your child's actions and feelings like an announcer describing a sports match (page 76).

Star charts

A tool for improving your older toddler's cooperation by making a daily recording on a little chart of a few specific behaviors you want to encourage (page 108).

Sweet spot

When talking to anyone who is upset, you'll be most successful having her feel respected and cared about if your tone of voice and facial gestures reflect about a third of the person's emotional intensity (page 47).

"Take-charge" consequences

Stronger penalties like time-out and giving a fine are the best way to quickly stop red-light behaviors (page 185).

Time-in

Feeding your child's meter with a little gift of your time and attention (page 99).

Time-out

A short period of isolation to put a halt to unacceptable behaviors (page 190).

Toddler-ese

A special language that's supereffective with upset toddlers, made up of three simple steps: short phrases, lots of repetition, and mirroring a bit of the child's feelings to connect with her emotional sweet spot (page 67).

Win-win compromise

Too many of us try to end conflicts with "I win . . . you lose" solutions. A better way to resolve disagreements (with your child or anyone else) is to find compromises where you *both* get some of what you want (page 163).

Yellow-light behavior

Annoying things your child says and does that you want to discourage (page 147).

"You-I" message

A valuable way of helping your child see *your* point of view by saying, "When *you* do . . . *I* feel. . . ." (page 54).

Index

About the Author

HARVEY KARP, M.D., F.A.A.P., is an assistant professor of pediatrics at the USC School of Medicine. He is also the creator of the national bestselling DVD and book *The Happiest Toddler on the Block* and *The Happiest Baby Guide to Great Sleep: Simple Solutions for Kids from Birth to Five Years*. Thousands of specially certified Happiest Baby educators teach his landmark ideas on baby calming and sleep in hospitals and clinics across North America and around the world. Dr. Karp is a nationally renowned expert in child development, children's environmental health, and breast-feeding. He lives with his wife in California. His adult daughter lives in New York.

happiestbaby.com

PAULA SPENCER is a writer and mother of four in Chapel Hill, North Carolina.